AMERICA

☆

Needs a Raise

Fighting for Economic Security

☆ **and** ☆

Social Justice

AMERICA

Needs a Raise

JOHN J. SWEENEY

PRESIDENT
OF THE AFL-CIO

with David Kusnet

HOUGHTON MIFFLIN COMPANY
BOSTON • NEW YORK
1996

For information about permission to reproduce selections
from this book, write to Permissions,
Houghton Mifflin Company, 215 Park Avenue South,
New York, New York 10003.

For information about this and other Houghton Mifflin
trade and reference books and multimedia products,
visit The Bookstore at Houghton Mifflin
on the World Wide Web
at http://www.hmco.com/trade/.

Library of Congress Cataloging-in-Publication Data
Sweeney, John.
America needs a raise : fighting for economic security
and social justice / John J. Sweeney, with David Kusnet.
p.   cm.
ISBN 0-395-82300-5
1. Trade-unions — United States. 2. AFL-CIO. 3. Labor
movement — United States. 4. Wages — United States.
5. Cost and standard of living — United States. 6. Income
distribution — United States. 7. Job security — United
States. I. Kusnet, David, 1951-   II. Title.
HD6508.S87 1996 96-21008
331.88'0973—dc20 CIP

Printed in the United States of America

Book design by Robert Overholtzer

BP 10 9 8 7 6 5 4 3 2 1

Acknowledgments

I am grateful beyond words to the more than thirteen million men and women of the AFL-CIO, whom I have the honor to represent. And every day I benefit from the wise advice and unshakable commitment of Rich Trumka, Linda Chavez-Thompson, and every member of the AFL-CIO Executive Council who has accepted the challenges that are presented in this book.

The idea for this book originated with Steve Fraser, my editor at Houghton Mifflin. Steve is a labor historian in his own right, the author of an outstanding biography of Sidney Hillman, and a leader in the effort to restore the alliance between the labor movement and liberal intellectuals.

From start to finish in the preparation of this book, Ray Abernathy, Jon Hiatt, Nancy Mills, Denise Mitchell, Karen Nussbaum, Gerry Shea, and Bob Welsh offered indispensable help in framing the issues and making the case.

At the AFL-CIO, Marc Baldwin, Elizabeth Barnes, Richard Bensinger, Michael Byrne, Larry Engelstein, Richard Foster, Arlene Holt, Peggy McCormick, Angela Morris, Peter Rider, Steve Rosenthal, and Kathy Smith are among many who were very helpful.

People from many unions of the AFL-CIO helped gather

and verify information about their unions and industries. These helpful people include Matt Bates, Paul Booth, Larry Cohen, Dave Elsila, David Hoffman, Gary Hubbard, Frank Joyce, Paul Krell, Patrick Lacefield, Jeffrey Miller, Jo-Ann Mort, Joyce Moscato, Margaret Peisert, Peter Pocock, Magda Lynn Seymour, Dave Snapp, Mary Sneden, Nancy Stella, and Matt Witt. They are not responsible for any shortcomings in this book.

Larry Mishel, Richard Rothstein, and Ruy Teixeira, of the Economic Policy Institute, and Geoff Garin and Guy Molyneux of Garin-Hart Research, made valuable comments on early drafts of several chapters. This book also draws on the findings of Representative David Obey and Scott Lilly of the Democratic Policy Committee, as well as reports by Citizen Action and public opinion surveys by Garin-Hart Research, Stanley Greenberg, Mark Mellman, and Celinda Lake.

Carter Wright helped compile much of the research and conducted several interviews. Jeffrey Lerner and Amy Mayers were helpful in compiling videotapes of hearings, demonstrations, and other public events. Carter Wilkie helped verify the details of President Clinton's trip to Ireland. Victoria VanSon also helped to obtain and verify information.

At Houghton Mifflin, Frances Apt, Chris Coffin, Robert Overholtzer, Becky Saikia-Wilson, and Lenora Todaro were very helpful.

And, of course, I will be grateful to you, the reader, if you join the effort to win working Americans a better deal and a stronger voice.

— John J. Sweeney

Contents

This book is for all Americans who are
worried about disappearing jobs, shrinking
paychecks, vanishing health care, plundered
pension plans, and the sense that their
work is no longer respected and rewarded.

The earnings due to the AFL-CIO from
the sale of this book will go into a special
America Needs a Raise Fund
to help working Americans organize for
higher living standards and a stronger
voice on their jobs.

CHAPTER I

It Doesn't Have to Be This Way

THIS BOOK is for Maria Herrera and Bill Dameron.

Maria Herrera works as a janitor in office buildings in downtown Washington, D.C. She cleans up after lawyers and lobbyists who make hundreds of thousands of dollars a year writing loopholes into the laws. She earns $6.20 an hour. That's less for a whole week scrubbing floors than many of the people whose offices she cleans get for just an hour of attending meetings. She lives with her husband in a one-bedroom apartment and sends $200 each month to her mother and her son in her native Honduras. And she worries that "with what I'm making, I may not be able to help support my family."

Bill Dameron has worked for a fueling company at Dulles Airport in northern Virginia for twenty-one years. His job is putting the fuel in airplanes — and that takes a lot more skill than you and I need to fill up our cars at the self-service station. Bill knows the individual planes, their structure, and their fueling requirements. And he has specialized skills, such as balancing the fuel load properly among the various tanks on the wings and in the belly of the plane. Travelers bet their lives on the quality of his work. But even though he keeps taking on new responsibilities, he works longer hours and takes home less in real wages than he did fifteen years ago. "Workers like me have been on the losing end for too long," he says.

Paychecks and Power

Maria and Bill understand the problem that's at the heart of so much anger and anxiety in our country: America needs a raise.

When you factor in rising prices for food, housing, health care, and other necessities, most Americans are working for less than they earned in 1979. They are more productive than ever. But their productivity hasn't been rewarded with higher wages.

Instead, corporate America is converting productivity gains into higher profits, skyrocketing executive salaries, and a speculative boom on Wall Street. At the same time, profitable companies are wiping out tens of thousands of jobs — and finding ways to skim off money that's supposed to be set aside for their employees' pensions. The result is the most lopsided distribution of wealth since just before the Great Depression.

To stay even, most families are working longer and harder. Even mothers of young children who'd rather stay home with their kids are taking jobs outside the home. Fathers — and mothers, too — are working overtime or taking second jobs. More teenagers are working after school. But, still, their families are going deeper into debt. As Americans struggle without reward, people wonder whether hard work is still valued. With less time to spend with their families, people worry whether their children are getting the attention they need and deserve.

The problem isn't just money. It's a sense of powerlessness — and voicelessness — in a new economy where the old rules no longer apply. Traditional ties of loyalty between employers and employees have been cut, and too many working people know they can't count on regular raises — or even on secure jobs. Working Americans know they have little say over their jobs, their paychecks, or even how they divide their time between earning their livings and raising their children.

Without a voice in their lives and livelihoods, many people are listening to angry, sometimes hateful voices — Rush Limbaugh, Patrick Buchanan, and others who urge the frustrated middle class to blame their problems on immigrants, minorities, and poor people who are having an even harder time. These voices fill a vacuum — a dangerous vacuum. In politics, in the media, and in most workplaces, nobody's speaking for working men and women. Nobody's explaining what's happening to their jobs and incomes. Nobody's fighting for their right to a secure future and a fair share of the wealth they produce. And history teaches that democracy is in big trouble when most people think: "Nobody cares about me. Nobody listens to me. And nobody speaks for me."

That is why I stood with Maria Herrera and Bill Dameron on a sweltering afternoon in June 1995 in a park a few blocks away from the White House. We were beginning a fight for the future of the institution that should speak for working people — the labor movement. I was kicking off my candidacy for president of the AFL-CIO, the federation that includes seventy-eight national unions, with more than thirteen million working men and women as members.

I believed the AFL-CIO and its future were worth fighting

for because, for all its shortcomings, the labor movement is the only force in society that expressly represents working families. And the AFL-CIO, in particular, has the potential to be a strong, influential, and respected voice not only for its members but for all working Americans. That is why it was worth fighting the first contested election in the federation's history. We were challenging entrenched traditions. But, more important, we were challenging the sense inside and outside the labor movement that there was little we could do to reverse the sliding standard of living for working Americans and the increasing polarization in our society.

We were concerned that the labor movement was becoming too weak to help raise the wages of workers like Maria or rebuild the living standards of workers like Bill. We believed that, with workers and their families hurting as never before, the labor movement must respond as never before. It was time to raise our voices, powerfully and persuasively, to restore respect for working Americans and the work they do.

During the campaign, I traveled across the country, from a steel mill in Pennsylvania, to a picket line in Detroit, to a protest march in Los Angeles. I listened to and learned from men and women who are having a hard time making ends meet. It is for them that I fight every day, now that I serve as president of the AFL-CIO. This book is for Maria, Bill, and every American who is worried about disappearing jobs, shrinking paychecks, vanishing health care, plundered pension plans, and the sense that their work is no longer respected and rewarded. And it's for everyone else who's concerned about the growing gap between the rich and the rest of us — and what it means for our values, our society, and our democracy. If you picked up this book because it's about "social justice" as well as "economic security," then this book is for you.

When I listen to working people complain that their lives are getting tougher and nobody speaks for them, I think, "It doesn't have to be this way." It isn't only impersonal forces like trade and technology — it is flesh-and-blood people in plush executive offices who make the decisions that drive down our living standards and divide our society. For instance, there's Albert ("Chain Saw") Dunlap, the former chief executive officer of Scott Paper, who cut eleven thousand jobs in 1994 — and then received $100 million in pay and stock profits and other perks when he merged the company with Kimberly Clark.[1] The problem is that the "Chain Saw" Dunlaps have too much power, and the rest of us have too little.

I am writing this book to ask you to join the fight for every American's right to contribute to — and share in the gains of — a growing economy. Part of the challenge is the effort we began last summer: to rebuild and revitalize the American labor movement. As unions speak for a greater proportion of the workforce, and as we mobilize our members more effectively, we will be able to improve their pay and prospects and help them win more of a voice in decisions where they work.

But, even more important, I see a stronger labor movement as the core of a larger effort to achieve economic security and social justice. This movement will unite working Americans, and all Americans of good will, across the lines of color, class, and culture that divide us today.

That kind of common purpose built the world's strongest economy and the world's largest middle class in the era after World War II. Most Americans lived by common values and shared understandings — a social compact, if you will — that guided our country through a period of economic growth and shared prosperity. Business, labor, and government all agreed that working people were entitled to a fair share of the wealth they produced. Our economy benefited because high wages generated strong consumer demand. And our social fabric and our political process were strengthened because upward mobility made Americans more confident and cohesive. Growing wages paid for important investments, from public education to the interstate highways.

Strong unions made all this possible. The labor movement won higher wages and better benefits for workers in the industries where we were strongest. By doing that, we set the pace for the rest of the economy. Because workers had more power at the bargaining table, they were able to share in the gains of their growing productivity. The union contract was the strongest guarantee for the social contract.

And unions were a powerful force for economic security and social justice, not only at the bargaining table but in the political process. In the hallway near my office at the AFL-CIO, there is an exhibit of a hundred pens that President Lyndon Johnson gave the federation's first president, the legendary George Meany. Johnson had used the pens to sign historic social legislation that the labor movement had helped push to passage, including civil rights, voting rights, Medicare, Medicaid, student loans, and improvements in Social Security.

That was thirty years ago. Since then, the economy has been transformed by new technologies, global trade, and the deregulation of leading industries. All these changes have been analyzed exhaustively, but one important trend has gone unnoticed: the shift in the balance of power between the people who do America's work and the people who control their lives and livelihoods. In the high-tech global economy, investment capital can cross the earth in an instant, with a keystroke on a computer. While business can pack up and move anywhere, American workers are committed to this country — and to their communities as well because of their ties to family, friends, and neighbors.

Under the best of circumstances, the mobility of wealth and the immobility of workers would produce an imbalance of power. Workers' leverage is further reduced by the decline of the labor movement, from a third of the workforce forty years ago to 16 percent today. Workers suffer from that loss of power at every level where the future of their jobs and paychecks is decided — from their workplaces to the corridors of political power.

Since the 1970s, employers have met the challenge of global competition, not with American teamwork and American know-how but by driving down labor costs. And, too often, unions have lacked the power to prevent management from taking the low road. Labor's loss of power has been reflected, too, in a growing meanness in public policy. By the 1980s, Presidents Ronald Reagan and George Bush were using their pens to sign tax cuts for the wealthy and cuts in social programs for everyone else. Even under a friendlier president, Bill Clinton, working people aren't gaining ground, although they have been protected from the worst assaults of a Republican Congress. For most wage earners, the past quarter-century has been "the winter of our discontent."

On that summer day last year, when I talked about a new voice for workers like Maria Herrera and Bill Dameron, I meant a stronger labor movement that will speak for working people where it counts — in their workplaces, at the bargaining table with management, in the halls of Congress, on the airwaves, and in communities across the country.

I offer in this book a vision of a revitalized labor movement that will reach out to and raise up the new American workforce: those whose jobs have been created by the trends that are transforming the economy, as well as those whose security is being swept away. I want to build a labor movement that will address working people's needs not only for a decent standard of living but also for fulfilling jobs in making products or providing services in which they can take pride.

Our ultimate goal is a new social contract, by which workers will share not only in prosperity but in power. The old social contract that made America so successful during the postwar era was based on a simple but profound truth: for the economy to grow and prosper, working people must be able to buy the goods and services they produce.

The new social contract that America needs to survive and thrive in this era is based upon another fundamental fact: we live in a new economy. Small differences in quality spell success or failure in the ultra-competitive global marketplace. That is why, now more than ever, working people need a voice in improving the quality of the goods they produce and the services they provide. Just as growing paychecks for workers contributed to American consumer demand in the old economy, greater power for workers can contribute to American competitiveness in the new economy.

On that sweltering summer afternoon, we took on a tough job: building a new social movement and forging a new social contract. But I know that working people can improve their conditions and their country because I've seen it happen in my own life. I came of age in the America of the old social contract. As with many of my generation, it took me from a tenement to a college classroom to what my father would have called "indoor work without heavy lifting." Maybe because I wanted to help people who grew up in circumstances like my own, I've spent my adult life in the labor movement.

For the past twenty-five years and more, I've found myself struggling against the current in a cruel new economy that seems intent on driving people down and driving them apart. My goal is to leave a legacy similar to the advantage my own generation enjoyed: a social movement and a social contract that will once again lift Americans up and bring us together.

A Rising Tide

I want to tell you a little more about the world that shaped me. An immigrant family. A working-class neighborhood. A church that cared about our daily lives as well as our immortal souls. And a labor movement that lifted my father's spirit as it raised his wages. That world is long gone, but what's worth remembering are values that have stood the test of time, especially the sense that we were put on earth to care for one another and work together for a larger purpose. That spirit can see us through the age of fax machines and modems as surely as it guided us through the era of trolleys and typewriters.

I grew up in the Bronx, in a happy home with two sisters and a brother. Sure, the Bronx has always had its share of poverty and pain, but it's also filled with history and hope. Of all the places on earth, it's one of an honored handful whose name is always preceded by "the." There's *the* Vatican, there's *the* Hague, and there's *the* Bronx. The people who gave it that noble name must have known it was going to be a special place.

Literally and figuratively, the Bronx is a bridge between a

city that's a port of entry for newcomers from all over the world and the nation where they hope to make a new life. As I like to remind friends who come from Manhattan, Brooklyn, Queens, and Staten Island, the Bronx is the only borough of New York City that isn't on an island but is part of the North American continent.

The Bronx has always been a pack-a-lunch and take-the-subway-to-work kind of place. Maybe that's why, of the four people who have served as president of the AFL-CIO, three of us (George Meany, Tom Donahue, and me) were born and raised in the Bronx. And the Bronx keeps turning out labor leaders. When I was a young man, my sister had a friend whose boyfriend was a heavy-equipment operator and was active in the Operating Engineers union. I got to know that fellow, Frank Hanley, as he rose in the ranks of his union, taking a little time off to attend Harvard University's trade union program. Now, he's national president of his union and a force for innovation, organizing not only in the construction industry but in health care as well.

I grew up in a community called Tremont, in St. Joseph's parish. My parents were Irish immigrants. My father was a bus driver on a route that wandered through the East Bronx. My mother was a domestic worker who came home every evening after cleaning other families' homes. In our modest walk-up apartment, we could hear the sounds of the street and smell our neighbors' cooking. Three things were central to our lives: church, family, and union. Without the church, there would have been no hope of redemption. Without the family, there would have been no love. And without the union, there would have been no food on the table.

My father was a loyal member of the Transport Workers Union — the TWU. Its president was Mike Quill, a colorful character who inspired his troops and often intimidated the management officials he faced across the bargaining table. TWU contracts expired at the stroke of midnight on New Year's Eve — and Quill would never rule out a strike until the ink was dry on a new agreement. So, early in the evening, New Yorkers would go out to celebrate, without knowing whether the subways would be running to take them home after midnight.

Quill spoke with an authentic Irish brogue; in fact, it was thicker than many I heard years later when I visited Dublin and Derry. Some cynics said his accent got heavier over the years, and that he'd really pour it on when his audience would appreciate it most. I prefer to think that great occasions inspired him to speak with inflections appropriate to an actor, a poet, or a rebel — and he was all three, and more.

I saw what the union meant for my father. It won him the wage increases that let him buy a home for his family. It won him a few extra days of vacation to spend with our family on the beach at Rockaway — at the other end of the city, in faraway Queens. When we took those vacation days, my father would say, "God bless Mike Quill. God bless the union."

So, even as a kid, I was fascinated by the organization that helped my father hold his head a little higher. I used to go to union meetings with him. I was intrigued by the debate, the votes, and, at crucial moments, the almost spiritual bond between people preparing for something close to battle. Even as a youngster, I could see how the members, who came to meetings wearied from long hours at work, seemed to gain energy from each other as the meetings went on.

Most of all, I loved to watch Mike Quill in action. One time, he was fighting with the city's chief executive, an unprepossessing fellow named Vincent Impellitteri. So Quill debated an empty chair reserved for His Honor the Mayor. "Where is Impy?" Quill kept asking. The members loved the show — and the sense that together they could fight City Hall.

Looking back on those days, I see that I learned how the union can be more than a mechanism for raising wages and resolving grievances; it can be a creative social movement. In the union hall, as at church, I had the sense that a person's dignity could flourish in a climate of fellowship and respect.

At those meetings, someone always made this point: what working people win at the bargaining table, we can lose in the political process. So, as a teenager, I plunged into politics.

I was fortunate to come along when politics depended on people, not just on money and the media. I remember one Saturday afternoon, just before Election Day early in the 1950s, when I was tooling around the Bronx in a sound truck, run by a couple of TWU bus drivers. We stopped at a shopping center, near a station on the elevated train line, and one of the older guys said to me, "Kid, why don't you take the microphone for a while?"

Now, the first mistake an inexperienced person makes with a microphone is to holler into it. That's what I did — and I heard my own voice, raucous and distorted, echoing back at me and scaring people away. So I settled down and started speaking in more measured tones. Sometimes, people tell me I'm a little too soft-spoken for a public speaker. My low-key speaking style may be an overreaction to my first encounter with a microphone.

Years later, after my family moved across the city line to Yonkers, I became a candidate myself — for Democratic district leader. I got my family, friends, and neighbors to ring doorbells for me, and I won the election. Much more impor-tant, I met the woman who became my wife. Maureen Power had gone to school with my sisters, and, after coming home from her job as a New York City schoolteacher, she would go out with them to ring doorbells. A while after the election, we got married. It was my most successful campaign.

My parents believed their four children could better them-selves through education — and, as usual, they were right. I attended Cardinal Hayes High School in the Bronx and Iona College in New Rochelle, where I majored in economics. Early in my high school years I spent a summer caddying at a country club in Yonkers. One Saturday morning in June, I participated in my first strike. The caddies were demanding a pay increase of seventy-five cents for every bag we carried, so we stopped work at the bottom of a hill on the golf course. After a while, the golfers understood we were serious, and they sent a committee to negotiate with us. We got our full seventy-five-cent-a-bag increase.

Later, to earn money for college, I worked summers at the Gate of Heaven Cemetery in Westchester County. It's where the legendary baseball great Babe Ruth was buried, and peo-ple would come to see his gravesite. My younger brother Jim also worked there. He used to remind me that I got the easier jobs — not digging the graves but filling them in after funer-als. Years later, automation would wipe out some of the jobs I did. But other tasks I tackled will be around as long as young people work with their elders. Often, I was a "gofer"; the older guys would send me out for things. But I was proud that at last I was part of the adult world of work. And I picked up my first union card as a member of Local 365 of what is now the Service Employees, the union I later led as national president.

In high school, at college, and, years later, at the old Xavier Labor School in Manhattan, headed by Fathers Philip Carey and John M. Corridan, who was portrayed by Karl Malden in the film *On the Waterfront,* I studied Catholic social teaching. In many ways, I learned a more detailed version of the values I'd been taught at home. Since men and women are created in God's image, their dignity must be respected. Working people have the right to a living wage — in fact, we used to say that breadwinners should earn a "family wage" so that they could support their households. And though there will always be some churning in the economy, working people should not be cast aside like disposable parts when the last drop of energy and effort has been wrung out of them. Recently, the United States Catholic Bishops said it all: "The economy exists for the human person, not the other way around."[2]

Human dignity demands that workers have a voice on the job, and the papal encyclicals we studied recognized the role of unions. Several priests and teaching brothers, particularly Father Philip Carey, of the Xavier Labor School, taught me a lesson I try never to forget: a union must be a movement and a mission, not a business or a bureaucracy. In particular, they taught that organizing new members is not only an institutional necessity but an ethical imperative. It is a practical example of the fortunate helping their less fortunate sisters and brothers. I stress the lessons of Catholic social teaching because these views shaped my thinking, certainly not because they are the only course to a commitment to the labor movement. Over the years, I have been struck by how many in the movement have been influenced by the teachings of their own traditions — from the prophets of the Old Testament, to the social gospel of modern Protestantism, and the determination of the African-American churches to help people make "a way out of no way." Whenever I hear the voices of prejudice and privilege claim scriptural sanction for their views, I wonder how they managed to read the Bible without coming across the words "justice" and "love."

I'm not saying that people who believe, as I do, in the traditional values of work, family, and faith must support the labor movement in everything we do. But I do believe that for people to live decent lives — with lasting commitments to their families and neighbors — they need some security. The plant closings of the 1980s and the corporate downsizings of the 1990s have cut millions loose from their livelihoods. Surely this did at least as much harm to families and communities as all the violent TV shows and raunchy movies that Hollywood could churn out, even if they ran their studios around the clock, like steel mills in the boom years.

After college, I landed a job as a market researcher with IBM at their market research center in White Plains. It was during the 1950s, at a time when large corporations were confident and secure as never before — and never since. We wore the corporate uniform: white shirt, dark suit, subdued tie, black shoes. And we did as we were told. I often wonder what happened to the project they assigned me: to explore the market for "small computers." What they had in mind wasn't the desktop personal computer, which revolutionized the industry thirty years later, but the small mainframe computer for use by private companies. It would be the size of a credenza and would work in tandem with a keypunch operation and a printer. Altogether, the system would take up a medium-sized room. That was the 1950s notion of a "small computer."

After a short while at IBM, I was offered a job as a researcher for the International Ladies Garment Workers Union

(ILGWU). It meant taking a pay cut, from $90 to $60 a week — but I grabbed it. It put me where I wanted to be: helping working people make their lives a little better. When I gave notice to IBM, I told them my younger brother had a similar educational background and, sure enough, they hired Jim. He stayed with the company for more than thirty years, until he took early retirement just before a major "downsizing" decimated IBM's workforce. I sometimes wonder whether IBM would have held on to its position in the industry — and tens of thousands of employees would have held on to their positions at IBM — if the company had shown more imagination in exploring the market for "small computers."

I've taken the time to tell you my story because it's typical of the lives Americans led in the years after World War II. Many of us remember them as "the best years," not just because so many moved up, but because Americans were moving forward together. Recently, I read the autobiography of a better-known product of the Bronx, who also grew up in an immigrant family. In words that echo in my own experience, he tells how the old social contract helped the sons and daughters of the working class climb the ladder of success:

> I was born a New Deal, Depression-era kid. Franklin Roosevelt was a hero in my boyhood home. Government helped my parents by providing cheap public subway systems so that they could get to work, and public schools for their children, and protection under the law to make sure their labor was not exploited. My mother's International Ladies Garment Workers Union, with its right to bargain collectively secured by law, also protected her. . . . I received a free college education because New York taxed its citizens to make this investment in the sons and daughters of immigrants and the working class.[3]

The man who wrote those words is General (retired) Colin Powell. He recently engaged in the ultimate act of upward mobility: he became a Republican. But I was reassured to read that he hasn't forgotten the place he came from and the programs that helped him become an authentic American hero. The Powells, the Sweeneys, and millions like us were fortunate to come of age at a time when business, labor, and government upheld the social contract.

Working people knew that if they got up every morning and did well on their jobs, they could earn a better life for themselves and a better chance for their children. Strong unions like the ILGWU and the TWU helped Colin Powell's parents and my own get a fair share of the wealth they produced. Business people knew that if they paid their workers fairly and plowed some of their profits back into their communities, they could count on loyal employees and loyal consumers. For companies back then, good citizenship was good business. And our leaders in government understood that, as President Kennedy said, "A rising tide lifts all boats." They saw their purpose as raising the standard of living for all, not accumulating enormous wealth for just a few.

Under the postwar social contract, most people had good reason to believe that their work was respected and rewarded. And their jobs did not devour their lives: people worked to live — they did not live only to work. It was possible for wage earners to support their families with their paychecks from one good-paying job, particularly if the pay was union scale. Because working people had more time to spend as they chose, they were able to devote more time to their families and to their communities. Voluntary organizations flourished, from PTAs and Little Leagues to church and synagogue groups, scout troops and political clubs, local unions and professional associations. City neighborhoods and small towns were humming with the activities that we think of as typically American.

Lord knows, America wasn't perfect. But Americans entered the 1960s with the confidence that we could keep moving forward together. It was typical of the times that John F. Kennedy's campaign tune was a popular song entitled "High Hopes." And the struggles for civil rights and women's rights were not only an answer to injustice but also an expression of the optimism of the America of the postwar social contract. It was a time when we believed everything was possible.

Against the Current

When I went to work for the International Ladies Garment Workers Union, I saw a social movement that lifted working people up — and the economic trends that were dragging them down. Founded at the turn of the century, mostly by Jewish and Italian immigrants, the ILGWU had raised generations of workers from sweatshop conditions to a measure of middle-class security. By the time I went to work for it, the ILGWU was involved in much more than bargaining contracts and resolving grievances. It sponsored health centers, housing developments, and educational programs for garment workers and other working-class New Yorkers. Years later, it pioneered in paid advertising to spread labor's message — you probably remember the TV spots where real-life garment workers sang, "Look for the union label."

The ILGWU's president, from 1932 to 1966, was David Dubinsky, another larger-than-life labor leader, although he stood little more than five feet five inches tall. His Yiddish accent was as vivid as Mike Quill's brogue, and when the two disagreed about the fine points of progressive politics, the debate was fast, furious, and free-wheeling. DD and his counterpart from the men's clothing workers' union, Sidney Hillman, had helped build a lasting partnership between the labor movement and Franklin D. Roosevelt's New Deal. In fact, some Republicans charged that before FDR made a major move, he would "clear it with Sidney."

As a staffer for the ILGWU, I would help locals prepare for contract talks and members prepare for hearings on grievances or unemployment insurance or disability claims. I heard their stories, and I could feel the winds of change that were sweeping away much of the American clothing and textile industry. Employers were leaving the union strongholds of the Northeast and Midwest for low-wage, nonunion areas in the South and Southwest. Some companies went even farther in their search for cheap labor — to Central and South America and Asia, where workers could be put to work for pennies an hour. That was why, since 1960, America lost hundreds of thousands of jobs in the textile and clothing industries, and their unions lost two-thirds of their members.

By the 1980s, history took a tragic turn. Partly because of the pressure of nonunion conditions in the South and cheap-labor competition throughout the world, sweatshops were appearing again in New York, Los Angeles, and other major cities. In 1995, Americans were shocked when illegal immigrants from Thailand were freed from prisonlike conditions at a clothing factory in El Monte, California. Their plight was part of the larger problem of sweatshops, which routinely violate laws about the minimum wage, overtime, and health and safety. That is why it was great news when the ILGWU and the Amalgamated Clothing and Textile Workers Union merged in 1995 to found a new organization, appropriately called UNITE (the Union of Needletrades, Industrial, and Textile Employees). Under the leadership of its president, Jay Mazur, UNITE is devoting substantial resources to organize garment and textile workers, from the sweatshops of New York and Los Angeles to the mill towns of the South. On the day after I was elected president of the AFL-CIO, I led a march down Seventh Avenue to the heart of New York's garment district, where a new generation of immigrant workers is in need of union representation. I felt that I was returning to familiar territory — and resuming work on unfinished business.

I had left the ILGWU in 1961 to work for the union I'd joined years earlier as a working member, which was then called the Building Service Employees. I seemed to be following a path that foreshadowed the trends in the American economy — away from manufacturing and toward the service sector. But, really, I was just following a friend's advice.

The friend was Tom Donahue, whom I'd met years before at labor events in New York. Tom was a graduate of Manhattan College, which has a fierce rivalry with Iona in basketball. So it may have been in the cards that, decades later, we would be rivals for the presidency of the AFL-CIO. But nothing will ever diminish my respect for Tom. He is a man of many talents: a thinker, a writer, and a public speaker. And he is as decent and dedicated a trade unionist as any I've met.

When I met Tom Donahue, he was with Local 32B of the Building Service Employees, which represents building service workers throughout the city. In 1961, Tom was moving to Washington to work for the national union, where he would be an early architect of its growth. He was looking for someone to replace him as contract director for Local 32B, and recommended me to David Sullivan, who was leaving the local to become president of the national union.

Just as my work with the ILGWU had given me a glimpse of how globalization was transforming the economy, Local 32B let me see firsthand how new technologies were wiping out jobs. Elevator operators were one of the largest groups within the local, providing much of its leadership. But by the early 1960s, elevator automation had wiped out some twenty thousand jobs. In 1961, in a study of the impact of automation on elevator operators, Brother C. Justin, director of the Labor-Management Department at Manhattan College (and a mentor to Tom Donahue and me), concluded prophetically: "The social and economic impact of the disappearance of so many . . . jobs for our less skilled or less rugged . . . workers requires attention. Obviously, if the industry and the local citizens cannot combine to solve this problem, then the government must come to the aid of those less skilled or less rugged . . . workers who are in quest of work."[4]

At first, the union tried to stop the new elevators, citing "fatal accidents and the danger of muggings." By the 1960s, we devoted our efforts to retraining the displaced workers for new jobs. With funds from the federal, state, and city governments, we set up programs for teaching members English, mathematics, electricity, carpentry, and plumbing, among other subjects and skills. Yet, in spite of all we tried to do, there were always reminders of how much hurt there is among people who do difficult and dangerous jobs.

During the holiday season, we would deliver packages of gifts — turkeys or hams, cake or cookies — to the families of members who had been injured and were unable to work. I vividly remember one visit to the home of a member who'd been hurt on his job as a porter in a luxury apartment build-

ing in Manhattan. He lived in a modest apartment in the
Bronx, just north of Yankee Stadium. When I visited his
family on my way home to Yonkers one night, I was struck by
the fear on the faces of the worker, his wife, and their children. He'd been out on disability benefits for six months and
was hoping he'd be able to go back to work. But if he didn't
get better, what was the future for a grown man who earned
his living doing heavy lifting?

In 1976, I was chosen as president of Local 32B. It was our
nation's Bicentennial. But it was also an era of energy crises,
inflation and recession, and hard times for sectors of the
economy all the way from the auto industry to state and
local governments. Employers were beginning to play hard-
ball with labor, and we had to fight back with hard-nosed
bargaining and aggressive organizing. Less than eight weeks
after I took office, the apartment building owners hit us with
what would become a familiar weapon — a demand for cuts
in wages and benefits. We responded with a strike that won
substantial wage increases. It was the first of two citywide
strikes I would lead.

To build membership strength, we kept reaching out to new
groups of workers. In 1977, we merged with our sister local,
Local 32J, which mostly represented women building maintenance workers. That local had made headlines and history
years before, when it successfully demanded that all cuspidors
— unsanitary utensils for spit-out chewing tobacco and the
like — be removed from office buildings. By the 1970s, separate locals for men and women were an anachronism that our
union was well rid of, and we were much stronger standing
together than staying separate.

Together with another Service Employees local, Local 32B-
J launched an organizing drive among New York City home-

care employees that has brought almost twenty thousand workers into the union. For many members of our union, the home-care workers were friends, neighbors, and family members — the folks we saw when we went shopping on Saturdays or to church on Sunday. As the son of a domestic worker, I could identify with these home-care workers, who dedicate their lives to serving others and deserve a decent income and a voice in their jobs.

As we organized new workers and won them better pay and benefits, I was continually struck by a simple fact. Janitors, health-care workers, and taxi drivers, to name just a few groups, don't have to be low-wage workers. With a union, they can earn a decent living, with health coverage and pension plans, and help their children get an education and move ahead in life. Instead of depending heavily on social programs, these workers can be productive members of society, paying taxes and recycling their paychecks through the economy. When politicians talk about welfare reform, it seems to me that the first sensible step is to make work pay — and the best way to do that is to organize low-wage workers.

While we were scrambling in the rough-and-tumble world of labor relations in New York, our national union was organizing workers who had too often been exploited by their employers and overlooked by the labor movement. The union changed its name to the Service Employees International Union (SEIU), and it organized throughout the fast-growing service sector of the economy. Hospital workers, social workers, cafeteria workers, clerical workers, building cleaners, even workers at racetracks and bowling alleys — we organized them all. Most were women. Many were African Americans, Latinos, or Asian Americans. Some were recent immigrants.

Professional employees, in particular, were demanding not only economic security but more of a voice in decision making. Many had gone to work for government or in health care hoping to help people. Instead, they found themselves struggling against stifling bureaucracies and shrinking resources.

For instance, Pam Johnson, a registered nurse in Los Angeles, said, "I would like to think I am working for a hospital and not an investment corporation where a few individuals are building private fortunes. I became a nurse so I could support my family with dignity. My patients are not customers."[5]

These concerns were typical of a new generation of working women and men in the state, local, and federal governments, the schools, and the fast-growing service sector of the economy. Teachers, school aides, communications workers, hospital and nursing home employees, workers in supermarkets and department stores, and employees at every level of government all joined unions. In addition to the Service Employees, some of the fastest-growing labor organizations were the American Federation of State, County, and Municipal Employees (AFSCME), the American Federation of Teachers (AFT), the United Food and Commercial Workers (UFCW), and — outside the AFL-CIO — the National Education Association. For the past three decades, the labor movement's growth in the service sector and the public sector is what kept our membership totals stable, at a time when millions of jobs were wiped out in basic industries.

In 1980, at a convention in Manhattan, the delegates elected me as president of the SEIU. In my acceptance speech, I warned that the "radical, reactionary right" was "out to destroy the trade union movement." But I can't claim that I anticipated everything that the Reagan and Bush administrations would do to working Americans. With massive layoffs in manufacturing and emboldened employers breaking unions, overall union membership declined during the 1980s from nearly 22 percent of the total workforce to only about 18 percent.

One thing the Service Employees kept doing during that decade was *organize*. In addition to the difficult day-to-day work of organizing individual hospitals, nursing homes, or building complexes, we would often target entire corporations — even entire industries.[6]

For instance, in 1982, SEIU and the United Food and Commercial Workers took on the nation's largest nursing home chain — Beverly Enterprises. Beverly was typical of the giant corporations that were making health care a big and booming business. It swallowed up smaller nursing homes, often using little more than corporate debt to do so. Wall Street loved Beverly for its huge profits, but workers worried about low wages, dangerous working conditions, and dismal patient care. We went after Beverly with every weapon at our disposal. While local unions organized workers at the nursing homes one by one, their efforts were aided by a coordinated campaign strategy. What we did was tell the truth: patients as well as workers were suffering from substandard conditions.

For instance, more recently, a study of care at thirty-five Beverly nursing homes in Missouri from April 1991 through December 1993 by the AFL-CIO's Food and Allied Service Trades Department found inadequate staffing levels and incidences of improper restraint and sedation. At 70 percent of the homes that were studied, patients suffered from bedsores. Staff didn't have the time to help them move around in their beds or chairs, or to provide proper treatments for minor injuries such as blisters. According to a state inspector, at one

home a resident had an "enormous and gaping" bedsore that
hadn't been properly diagnosed or treated for more than a
month.[7]

Beverly Enterprises has also disregarded its employees'
rights. In a 1995 report, the General Accounting Office, the
investigative arm of Congress, listed Beverly among federal
contractors that have violated labor law. The report said
the National Labor Relations Board had found that Beverly discharged sixteen workers during union organizing campaigns at twenty-three facilities across the country and also
"took numerous unlawful actions to thwart union activity,
including threatening discipline against workers for union
activity."[8] In spite of this fierce opposition from the company,
the unions are continuing their efforts to help workers organize, emphasizing that patients and employees share a common
interest in improved health and safety conditions at the nursing homes.

We used similar tactics to rebuild our union's historic base
in the building services industry. As with workers in so many
other sectors of the economy, building service workers found
themselves up against cutthroat corporate giants. In city after
city, powerful real estate barons and huge multinational contractors were consolidating their control of the industry.
Their goals: to break unions and drive down wages.

Our answer was to make every contract battle into a campaign that would inspire our allies and embarrass our adversaries. We called the campaign Justice for Janitors. Our first
test came in Pittsburgh, where building service workers were
locked out of their jobs for two winter months when they
refused to take a 25 percent pay cut and loss of benefits. Up
against a business community led by the wealthy and powerful Mellon Bank, the union took its case to the public and

won support from working people and others of good will throughout the country. We persisted — and prevailed.[9]

Using media campaigns, mass demonstrations, and political pressure, Justice for Janitors won similar victories across the country. In 1990, in the glitzy office district of Century City, Los Angeles, striking janitors and their supporters stood their ground against an attack by baton-wielding police; scores of marchers were injured in the police riot, but the union eventually prevailed. I'll tell you more about Justice for Janitors toward the end of this book, when I'll sketch out a vision of how the labor movement can become a vibrant and powerful social movement.

On a fall day in 1992, more than eight hundred registered nurses at the Jackson Memorial Hospital in Miami voted to join the Service Employees. Their decision pushed our union over the million-member mark. The union's success was a signal to a beleaguered labor movement that if we dared to reach out to workers beyond our ranks, we could rebuild our strength and regain our soul. And the hopes we raised helped kindle the campaign Maria Herrera and Bill Dameron joined last summer: to build a movement that can raise the living standards and improve the lives of every working American.

The labor movement we envision will meet the needs of working Americans in today's economy. It will reach out to millions of working men and women, from health care to high tech. Through the strength of its numbers and the rightness of its cause, it will put pressure on corporate America to raise wages and secure their jobs.

But that's just the beginning. While I've spent my life helping low-wage workers get a raise, I understand that a revitalized labor movement will also need to give voice to working people's yearnings to make better products and provide better services. It will be a source of education and training, helping working people acquire the skills they need in the new economy.

And it will push for a share of power in corporate decision making, urging companies to invest in their workers and emphasize long-term improvements in quality instead of short-term windfalls in their bottom lines. Thus, it will help make companies more competitive and the economy more prosperous. Even more important, a revitalized labor movement will be the core and the catalyst for a new social movement extending well beyond our ranks, a movement that will push for public policies promoting economic security and social justice. And that movement itself will help bridge some of the racial and social gaps in our country and restore a sense of purpose to public life.

That's what we mean when we say, "America needs a raise." Working together, working Americans can regain a sense of purpose and power — and we can lift our spirits as well as our wages.

CHAPTER 2

Downsized Dreams

SOMETIMES, Eddie Neace and his dad talk about how times have changed.

When Eddie was growing up, his father, Roy, was a line inspector at the Square D electrical parts plant in the southern Ohio town of Oxford. Roy Neace was a union man, a member of the International Brotherhood of Electrical Workers. And he made good money — about $7 an hour in 1970, a wage that would buy as much as $21 an hour today. That was enough to support the entire family, and Eddie's mother stayed home with the kids until his younger brother started school.

Eddie's dad would buy a new car every two years or so. For vacations, he'd take the family on weeklong trips, to places like Disney World or Gatlinburg, Tennessee. And when Eddie was growing up, his folks never worried about health care, because Roy Neace's union contract provided comprehensive coverage.

A Lesser Life?

As for Eddie, he went to work for A-Mold, a Japanese-owned auto-parts company in nearby Mason, Ohio, in 1992. He was twenty-three, and he was married, with two young children.

But Eddie's starting wage was $7.03 an hour, just about the same pay his father had earned more than two decades before. The cost of living had risen 293 percent since then, so Eddie's paycheck was worth considerably less. So, even though they had young kids at home, Eddie's wife frequently took temporary jobs to help make ends meet. Until recently, Eddie drove a 1984 Chevette he'd gotten from his father. When it came to vacations, the most the family could afford was an overnight trip to Sea World, just outside Cleveland.

Health care was another headache for Eddie and his family. The company's health plan wouldn't pick up all the costs for the delivery and care of his third child in 1993. In fact, it took Eddie two years to pay off the bills himself.

With their take-home pay coming out to little more than $200 a week, and their health plan in urgent need of improvement, workers at A-Mold kept trying to organize a union. In 1995, they voted to join the United Auto Workers and bargained their first union contract. It raised wages over $1 an hour for the average worker and over $2 an hour for some of the lowest paid workers, and it improved the health plan. Still, Eddie Neace worried about workers in the new economy. "I was getting the same wage my dad had started out with twenty years ago," he said. "I just don't see why our generation should be the first to work for a less prosperous life than our parents had."[1]

Eddie Neace stands on the less fortunate side of a fault line. If you got your first full-time job before the mid-1970s, you began your working life in an America where incomes and opportunities were expanding. But if you joined the workforce after that time, you came of age in an America where wages were declining, and most people were working longer and harder just to stay even. This is especially true for the three-fourths of the workforce who do not have four-year college degrees, and it is increasingly true even for those who have completed college. Americans understand that, just about two decades ago, America made an historic shift away from an economy that valued working people.

A leading activist on working women's issues, Karen Nussbaum (who now heads the AFL-CIO's Working Women's Department), remembers a comment that a Milwaukee man made on a radio talk show several years ago. He said he had five children, with twenty years' difference in age between the youngest and the oldest. The older three have good-paying jobs and support their families. But the younger two have minimum-wage jobs and still live at home. "The difference isn't the kids — they're just as well educated, just as hardworking," he said. "The difference is the times."

When the Going Was Good

America emerged victorious from World War II with a commitment to help people get ahead. The GI Bill helped many of the returning veterans become the first in their families to go to college. FHA mortgages helped working-class families buy their first homes. And, for the first time in history, a majority of Americans identified themselves as "middle class."

It was a time when the economy grew, and most Americans shared in the expanding affluence. From 1947 through 1973, family incomes grew by an average of 2.4 to 3 percent a year, no matter where the family stood on the economic ladder. Every sector of society — the rich, the poor, and the middle class — saw its incomes roughly double during the three decades after World War II.

Now, I don't mean to romanticize the period from the end of World War II through the early 1960s. That era left America with the unfinished business of eradicating discrimination according to race and sex. And I have a friend, about ten years younger than I am, who says: "I hated the fifties. I didn't have any money. Nothing happened. And I was bored to death." But there was a sense then that business and government cared about ordinary families. Sure, one cabinet secretary in the Eisenhower administration said, "What's good for General Motors is good for America." But there was also an understanding that what was good for working people was good for America. Put money in people's pockets, and they'd be able to afford houses, cars, washing machines, and TV sets. Companies would make money, and the economy would keep humming along. And it did.

That commitment to paycheck economics was enforced by a strong labor movement. At their high-water mark, in the mid-1950s, unions represented 35 percent of all American workers and 80 to 90 percent of those in major industries, such as auto, steel, and coal mining. Workers and their unions had a strong voice in setting wages and benefits in manufacturing and construction, and their gains set the pace for the entire economy, as employers competed for good workers and tried to dissuade them from organizing unions. Thus, as American workers became more productive, they shared in the bounty they produced. From 1947 to 1973, American workers gave their companies an almost 90 percent increase in productivity. And, in return, their real wages — their earnings after inflation — increased by 99 percent.

When the going was good — as it was for almost three decades after World War II — Americans moved forward together.

The Incredible Shrinking Paycheck

Starting in 1973, the year when energy prices soared, living standards took what the economists Barry Bluestone and Bennett Harrison call "the great U turn." Workers' real wages stagnated, and have actually tumbled 11 percent since 1978.

The problem isn't that Americans aren't working well enough — their productivity has increased by 24 percent since 1979, a substantial increase, although not as great as in the years after World War II. The problem is that productivity gains haven't found their way into the paychecks of "nonsupervisory or production employees" — a fancy phrase for workers who don't tell other workers what to do. And that's 80 percent of the workforce. Hourly wages for nonsupervisory employees have fallen (in 1995 dollars) from $12.85 in 1978 to $11.46 in 1995. That's a drop of 11 percent — or more than a dime on every dollar you earn![2]

For years, workers without four-year college degrees — and they make up about 75 percent of the entire workforce — suffered the most. Now, the living standards of all but the most privileged are in peril. Think of the workers doing the jobs that keep America humming — making steel, assembling automobiles, building houses. Most of these workers are men whose formal education ended with their high school diplomas. Over the last twenty years, their real incomes dropped by at least 20 percent. The decline in blue-collar wages — for women as well as for men — is felt across the board. From 1979 to 1995, average weekly earnings dropped by 17 percent in construction, 16 percent in transportation, and 7 percent in manufacturing. Retail workers' earnings dropped by 22 percent.

As for college graduates — women and men alike — they increased their real hourly pay during the 1980s. But since 1987, they've lost ground, too; their hourly earnings declined by 2 percent. Meanwhile, at the bottom of the economic ladder, more than twelve million workers labor for poverty wages, usually without health coverage, pension plans, or other benefits. They are victims of a minimum wage that has been frozen at $4.25 an hour since 1991 and buys just two-thirds of what the minimum wage provided in the mid-1960s.

At today's minimum wage, a full-time worker earns only $8840 a year — $3350 below the poverty line for a family of three. According to 1991 wage data, 4.1 million workers earn the minimum wage. Another 2.6 million make between $4.26 and $4.67 an hour, and another 5.8 million earn between $4.70 and $5.14 an hour. In the past, poor people worked their way into the middle class. Now, middle-class working people fear that they're plunging into poverty.

In a recent issue of *The New Yorker*, Susan Sheehan profiled a hard-working Iowa family. Bonita and Kenny Merton live with their two sons in their small home in Des Moines. Kenny had an $11-an-hour job before the factory closed. In 1994, he made $17,239 hauling sand sacks. Bonita made $13,977 working full time at Luther Park Nursing Home. After fifteen years, she's paid $7.40 an hour, gets a ham at Easter, a turkey at Thanksgiving, $10 for her birthday, and $20 at Christmas. She pays $36 a month for health insurance, $28 a month for dental coverage, and gets no pension. Every year, they go deeper and deeper in debt, and they are losing hope of ever doing better. Kenny says, "There ain't no middle class any-more. There's only rich and poor."[3]

The Dwindling Benefit Package

Not only wages but fringe benefits, like health-care coverage and pension plans, are on a downward spiral.

From 1987 to 1994, a million people a year lost their health coverage. The share of workers under sixty-five with employer-paid health care dropped from 63 to 56 percent. And workers who have coverage are increasingly part of a new corporate system — managed care — which is only now starting to be regulated in important ways to protect quality and accountability.

As for pensions, *Business Week* recently noted that the share of workers covered by employer-paid pension plans declined six percentage points between 1979 and 1988. This may not sound like a lot, but, as with health insurance, the whole system is changing. There's an even more troubling shift from secure plans, with workers required to pay more for a more risky future. And, as the private pension system is eroded, the public system, Social Security, is also under attack. Recent proposals to privatize the system threaten to make retirement funds less secure for all Americans.

From health care to pensions, economic and political forces are threatening workers' security. And, as with so many other problems, declining unionization is linked to declining coverage.

The New Nomads

One reason that pay and benefits are declining is the growth in the number of workers in temporary, part-time, low-wage, insecure jobs, with little or no health care or pension rights and few labor protections.

Temps, part-timers, and "independent contractors" make up what's called "the contingent workforce." Their jobs have some things in common: low wages, a lack of health insurance and pension benefits, and few, if any, basic legal protections for their health and safety on the job, their retirement security, their right to overtime pay, and their right to organize unions and bargain with their employers.

Estimates of the total contingent workforce range from thirty million to thirty-seven million people, about 25 percent of the entire workforce. It has increased 193 percent from 1985 to 1995. A recent Conference Board survey of ninety-three major multinational companies found that the proportion with 10 percent or more contingent employees has swelled from 12 percent in 1990 to 21 percent in 1995. Significantly, the largest private employer in the country isn't IBM, General Motors, or even McDonald's but the temporary agency Manpower, Inc.[4]

Companies like to talk about how all these temps make their firms "flexible," allowing them to meet unexpected needs.

But what happens to these workers when they face predictable points on life's journey — a serious illness or injury, having children, or reaching retirement? Meanwhile, the growing number of temporary employees puts regular employees at a disadvantage in their dealings with their employers. As a forty-four-year-old New Jersey man, who works as a supervisor in a private company, explained:

> Just the way you see how the corporations are taking all their money and not distributing it to their workers, hiring temps, it seems to me that they're looking to get rid of their full-time

employees. And the rate of pay that they're hiring the new people coming in is going down instead of coming up. So I just think the whole system is going to be more for the top and less for the bottom.[5]

The Great Productivity Heist

Why aren't working Americans getting raises in pay and benefits? The most important, and most overlooked, reason is that American workers no longer share in the gains of their growing productivity.

In the first nine months of 1995, workers' productivity grew by 2.9 percent. But their skimpy wage gains were canceled out by increases in the cost of living, so their real wages didn't grow at all. This continued the trend of the past fifteen years, with real wages declining by 12 percent from 1979 through 1994, while productivity increased by 24 percent.

Instead of finding its way into workers' paychecks, increased productivity has boosted corporate profits, which jumped by 205 percent between 1980 and 1995, and executive salaries, which have soared by 499 percent since 1980.[6] Why are workers losing out on their productivity gains? The reason is simple: the balance of power between American workers and their employers is dangerously out of kilter.

By the balance of power, I mean more than who has the edge when labor and management square off at the bargaining table, although the relationship between unions and corporations can set the tone for the treatment of workers throughout the economy. I mean who has the upper hand in every matter that comes up between employers and employees — union or nonunion, blue collar or white collar. Do you have the confidence to walk into your boss's office and ask for a raise? Or are you so anxious about keeping your job that you're willing to settle for the pay and benefits you already have?

In today's economy, employers are calling all the shots. They can threaten to move jobs to low-wage areas in this country or to low-wage nations overseas. They can replace employees with computers or machines, or with workers who have been "downsized" out of their jobs at other companies. They can fire you with impunity if you try to organize a union. And if you belong to a union and go on strike, they can bring in someone else — a "permanent replacement" — to take your job.

As Larry Mishel of the Economic Policy Institute explains, "If everyone is afraid that the job they now have is the best job that they can get, because if they lose it they go to a worse job, then no one — white-collar worker, blue-collar worker, union or nonunion — is able to put any pressure on the employer."

Working Americans understand how the threat of downsizing gives employers ever more power over their employees. A forty-eight-year-old Wisconsin man, a systems analyst, explained:

> Companies are downsizing. There's a large workforce, and they're capable of taking anyone's job at any time. So companies have no incentive to give anybody any more. Basically, the feeling is, if you don't like it, there's the door, there's others out there. And they're right. So I don't see the average worker gaining anything in the foreseeable future.[7]

Employers' overwhelming power over their employees can result in inhuman conditions in the workplace. For instance, here is how a worker at a nonunion food-processing plant in the Midwest described conditions in his factory:

> I make $6.80 an hour. . . . About two thirds [of the employees] make less than $6.00 an hour. . . . We have no benefits, no health insurance, no meaningful pension, nothing, nothing to go on.
>
> And . . . we have no voice in this place. He [the manager] doesn't listen to anything we have to tell him. Example . . . five people came down with some kind of rash that they got off the sauce or something they were allergic to. Their skin started cracking, it started bleeding. He wouldn't even give them gloves to wear. . . . He told them if they wanted to go to the doctor, they had to go on their own and pay for it out of their own pocket.[8]

Of course, much of the loss in workers' bargaining power has come about because of the decline in the labor movement. From our peak in the mid-1950s, when we represented 35 percent of the workforce, unions declined to 28 percent in the mid-1970s — and now we number only 15 percent of the entire workforce and a mere 11 percent in private industry.

According to a study by the labor economist Richard Freeman of Harvard, the decline of organized labor accounts for as much as 20 percent of the increase in wage inequality. And, as *Business Week* reports, the decline in union representation was a "key reason" for the shrinkage of employee benefit packages during the 1980s, including the 7 percent decline in companies with health coverage for their workers and the 6 percent drop in companies with pension plans.[9]

Increasing Inequality

The great productivity heist means the benefits of economic growth are reaching a narrower and narrower segment of the population. And that produces more inequality in wages and wealth. The top 20 percent of households now get half the nation's total income. *U.S. News & World Report* warns of "a growing chasm of income inequality in America."[10]

That chasm is widest between the people who do America's work and the people who run America's corporations. The average annual pay for a chief executive officer of a large corporation — including salary, bonuses, and stock options — was almost $2.9 million in 1994. That's the equivalent of a weekly paycheck totaling $55,400!

Since 1980, while workers' real wages have fallen, total CEO pay rose by 499 percent. Back in 1960, the average CEO earned forty-one times more than the average worker. By 1995, the average CEO raked in 145 times more than the average worker. To get an idea of what this means, imagine that it's payday — and your boss is getting 145 paychecks the size of yours.[11]

Meanwhile, the inequalities in wealth are growing even greater than the inequalities in wages. From 1983 to 1989, the top 1 percent gained 62 percent of the increase in total wealth, while the next 19 percent got 37 percent. This left the rest of America — the remaining 80 percent — with only 1 percent of the gain. And from 1989 to 1992, the trend actually accelerated, with the wealthiest 1 percent grabbing 68 percent of the total gain.

This wildly uneven accumulation of wealth is making the United States the most unequal country in the entire industrialized world. The top 1 percent controls 39 percent of the wealth — compared with 26 percent in France, 25 percent in Canada, 18 percent in Great Britain, and 16 percent in Sweden.

Downsizing Jobs — and Paychecks

One reason wages are declining is corporate America's grab of workers' productivity gains. Another reason is the replacement of millions of secure, well-paying, often unionized jobs at major corporations with lower-paid jobs elsewhere in the economy. When major corporations downsize their employees out of jobs, they are often downsizing their paychecks for years to come.

All this was unimaginable when I took my first full-time job. When I worked for IBM in the mid-1950s, my co-workers were confident that, unless we messed up badly on the job, we were secure for life. After all, IBM was proud of its famous no-layoff policy. By the beginning of the 1980s, IBM was still proud that it offered loyal employees secure jobs. The personnel manual still said:

> In nearly 40 years, no person employed on a regular basis by IBM has lost as much as one hour of working time because of a layoff. When recessions come or there is a major product shift, some companies handle the workforce imbalances that result by letting people go. IBM hasn't done that, hopes never to have to. . . . It's hardly a surprise that one of the main reasons people like to work for IBM is the company's all-out effort to maintain full employment.[12]

Fifteen years later, reading that IBM personnel manual is like coming across an ancient archeological artifact. You have the sense that you're looking at something from an earlier civilization, with different values and folkways. Tens of thousands of career IBM employees, including my brother Jim, have been downsized or face early retirement.

Recently, I was reminded of how much things have changed. I attended a meeting of the Business Council, a group that brings together corporate executives, government officials, and leaders from other walks of life. It was in a posh Washington hotel. The food was excellent. The conversation was friendly. And I had to remember that they hadn't invited John Sweeney, the guy who grew up in the Bronx, put himself through college digging graves, and headed up a local union of janitors. They'd invited the president of the AFL-CIO — and that fellow happened to be me.

Looking at the other participants through an outsider's eyes, I realized that many of these well-dressed, well-spoken people had something in common: they represented major corporations — such as AT&T, Caterpillar, Eastman Kodak, General Motors, Nynex, Chemical Bank, McDonnell-Douglas, and my old employer, IBM — that had wiped out tens of thousands of their employees' jobs during a period of economic recovery.

The talk was civil, and the tone of the meeting was cordial — just like the warm spirit of that old IBM personnel manual. But the reality of what many of their companies were doing was very different indeed — cold and cruel, like a pink slip in a pay envelope. The *New York Times* recently published a major series on corporate downsizings which found that more than forty-three million jobs were wiped out in the United States from 1979 through 1995.[13]

These mass firings continued during the recovery from the most recent national economic recession of 1990–1991. In fact, in recent years, these major employers had mass firings:

- AT&T: 40,000 jobs (as originally announced)
- General Motors: 75,000 jobs
- Sears, Roebuck: 50,000 jobs
- U.S. Postal Service: 50,000 jobs
- IBM: 60,000 jobs (and one IBM employee who took early retirement rather than a layoff was my brother Jim)
- General Dynamics: 30,000 jobs
- Boeing: 30,000 jobs
- United Technologies: 14,000 jobs
- Martin Marietta: 11,000 jobs
- Chemical–Chase Manhattan: 12,000 jobs

The economy generated twenty-three million more new jobs than were lost between 1979 and 1995, but most of the victims of corporate downsizings ended up in lower-paying positions. Thus, Labor Department statistics reveal that only about 35 percent of these workers find new jobs that pay as well as or better than their old ones. And a study of some two thousand workers let go by RJR Nabisco showed that 72 percent found jobs but at an average of only 47 percent of what their old jobs paid.

A World Without Raises

The productivity heist. Corporate downsizings. And the temping of America. All these trends are creating a world without regular raises for most workers. According to a survey of three hundred large companies by the Association for Quality and Participation, 74 percent are dismantling traditional pay schemes that award annual increases to most employees.[14]

In 1994, despite earning $1.7 billion in profits, Mobil Corporation adopted a new pay plan, freezing all salaries, on the theory that most workers are already earning too much. As *Business Week* reported, the top brass decided: "The bottom half [of Mobil's workforce] is even more over market [so] Mobil plans to lay off most of this latter group and subcontract the work to lower-paying outside companies." Similarly, IBM is ladling out $5.8 million in bonuses for its top five executives. Chairman Louis V. Gerstner, who was paid a total of $12.4 million last year, is getting a bonus of $2.6 million. But the folks who answer the executives' phone calls, type their letters, and schedule their meetings won't be sharing in the good times. Executive secretaries have been told to expect salary cuts of up to 36 percent, starting in June 1996.

Decisions like these are making regular raises a thing of the past for most workers. A thirty-nine-year-old Georgia woman, who works as an account manager, said:

> With our company, it's primarily because we went into a new salary plan, that you have to basically walk on water to get a salary increase. So they're just making it a lot tougher on people. It [a pay increase] is not like it used to be, where it was just expected and you knew it was going to happen. You really have to kill yourself to get anything.[15]

In a recent study of mostly nonunion American workers conducted for the AFL-CIO, the public opinion analyst Stanley Greenberg found that 65 percent of the non-college-educated men and 58 percent of the women say they have gotten no raises in recent years or have seen their wages go down. "That is now the way the world works," Greenberg reported. "One does not get raises that matter, unless one works longer hours, a higher paying shift, or an additional job. But, while wages do not rise, bills do . . . so the measure of well-being in this new economy is 'making the bills.'"[16]

Family Speedup

In an economy without raises, Americans are sending more family members into the workforce, working longer hours, and plunging deeper into debt. By 1990, 59 percent of mothers with young children held jobs outside the home — compared with 45 percent in 1980.

Meanwhile, men and women are working more hours and frequently holding several jobs. For all workers, the average number of working hours per year grew by 5 percent between 1979 and 1989. In what Americans think of as the typical household — a husband, wife, and children all living under the same roof — the mother worked 32.3 percent more hours outside the home in 1989 than she'd done in 1979. And the largest increase in working hours was for mothers in low-income households. Meanwhile, according to recent studies by Juliet Schorr of Harvard University, paid time off — vacations, holidays, sick leave, and personal days — dropped 15 percent in the 1980s.

Americans are working not only longer hours but also more jobs. From 1979 to 1989, the number of workers with more than one job jumped from 4.7 million to 7.2 million. This trend inspired a grim joke that became legendary in the overworked America of 1995. A politician tells the well-dressed guests at a fund-raising dinner, "Over the past three years, our economy has created more than eight million jobs." A waiter mutters under his breath, "Yeah, and I have three of them."

All in all, as the labor economist Audrey Freeman says, Americans have become "the workingest people in the world." But the median household income is still stagnating. That is why so many families are running up the balances on their credit cards. From 1980 to 1989, outstanding consumer credit jumped from $631 billion (in 1994 dollars) to $936 billion. By the holiday season of 1995, consumer spending suffered because so many families had "maxed out" on their credit cards.[17]

Families Facing "the Time Famine"

Working families are hard pressed for money — and for time. Together, the financial squeeze and the "time famine" are taking a terrible toll on family life. To be sure, there are many reasons that Americans are getting married later, having children later, and buying their first homes later. But one reason for people postponing life's major commitments is that, without secure jobs and rising incomes, they lack faith in their futures.

Mature workers with children are bearing the brunt of corporate downsizings, with disastrous effects on their families. In a study released in 1994, the Harvard economist James Medoff found that male workers in what should be their prime earning years — from the age of thirty-five to fifty-four — are most likely to suffer permanent layoffs. For more than a million men a year, prolonged unemployment comes at a time when their financial and family responsibilities are the greatest. Facing this midlife economic crisis, or fearing that it's around the corner, makes many workers angry and alienated.

For men and women who hold on to their jobs, but are

working longer hours just to stay even, the lack of time can be as corrosive on family life as the lack of money. Counting overtime and commuting, the average man works 48.8 hours a week, the average woman 41.7 hours. But in today's world, for men as well as women, their obligations don't end when they come home from their jobs.

During the workweek, the average man spends two hours on chores and three hours with the children. On weekends, he spends 4.67 hours on chores and 7.01 with his children. And, reflecting the fact that women still shoulder heavier responsibilities at home, the average woman spends 2.6 hours on chores and 3.75 hours with the children during the workweek — and 5.36 hours on chores and 9.20 hours with the children on weekends.

That's why 50 percent more Americans than three decades ago describe themselves as "always rushed." Working women, in particular, are stressed out by the competing demands of jobs and families. A survey of 250,000 working women for the Women's Bureau of the U.S. Labor Department showed that almost 60 percent identified "stress" as their number one problem.[18]

Listen to working women describing their days. Marina Foley, a grocery buyer and mother of two daughters, nine and thirteen, in Tallahassee, Florida, shared her schedule from May 15, 1995:

> This morning my alarm went off at 5:45. I hit snooze and squeaked out another fifteen minutes. Put the coffee on and then walked the dog and fed him. Started a load of laundry. Emptied the dishwasher. Daughter #1 has a huge track meet at school, so she had to be driven today. I then head to work. . . . At 4:45 P.M., I leave work to rush home to my latch-key nine-year-old daughter. . . . I usually don't sit down until 10:30 P.M.

There really is so much more to it, but when I started writing it down, I got overwhelmed.[19]

Dorothy Hunter, a single mother of two children, works on the assembly line at a poultry plant in Canton, Mississippi. Here's how her day goes:

I get up at 5:45, start breakfast, and get dressed for work. I get the children up, make their bed, eat breakfast, and [get them] dressed for school to catch the school bus. We start work at 7:33 . . . lunchtime at 12:55. At 1:20, I got back on the line. We work to 8:00 P.M. or later. My children go to my mother's house after school. They wait until I get off work. Thank God for my mother — they already have eaten. I look over their homework. We take a bath and get ready for bed about 9:30 or 10:30 P.M. [It] all depends on the time I get off work.[20]

Another woman, who had been told that Bill Clinton would receive a copy of the study, said simply, "Just tell the president I'm tired."

With less time to spend with their families, parents worry about whether their children can lead normal and decent lives. Every extra hour the father and mother spend at work is time they can't spend helping with the homework, coaching Little League or soccer practice, reading bedtime stories, or teaching life's daily lessons on the difference between right and wrong.

The public opinion analyst Celinda Lake explains: "For many voters, it is economic stress that has fueled a decline in values. Parents must spend so much time fighting for economic survival that they cannot spend the time necessary to teach children values and to protect them from the chaos around them."[21]

A parent from Raleigh, North Carolina, said:

I'm concerned about a breakdown in the family as far as values. I don't know whether it's due to families where both husband and wife and maybe a child need to be working outside the home in order to maintain some semblance of a lifestyle — not an extravagant one but just a lifestyle.[22]

People who have little time for their own families have even less time to spare for their communities. That is an important reason that civic activity is declining across America. Professor Robert Putnam of Harvard, the author of the influential article "Bowling Alone," wrote:

> Surveys of average Americans . . . in which they recorded every single activity during a day — so-called time budget studies — indicate that since 1965, time spent on informal socializing and visiting is down (perhaps by one-quarter) and time devoted to clubs and organizations is down even more sharply (by roughly half). Membership records of such diverse organizations as the PTA, the Elks Club, the League of Women Voters, the Red Cross, labor unions, and even bowling leagues show that participation in many conventional voluntary associations has declined by roughly 25 percent to 50 percent over the last two or three decades.[23]

With America becoming a nation of hurried, harried loners, our sense of community is being replaced by suspicion and hostility. When neighbors seem like strangers, strangers can seem like enemies.

The Loss of Loyalty

Our most cherished values — loyalty, the work ethic, and faith in the future — are being challenged not only in our families

and communities but in the workplace itself. For the past half
century Americans have believed that if they learned a skill,
found a job, and did right by their employers, they would be
rewarded with secure livelihoods and rising living standards.
Now, nothing seems so certain.

In a survey conducted by the *Chicago Tribune,* 64 percent
of Illinois voters disagreed with the traditional American view
that "a good education, job skills, plus hard work are usually
all it takes to achieve a good life today."[24] American achievement has always depended on the confidence that studying
hard and working hard will be rewarded. Without that confidence, will Americans make the effort to build better lives
for themselves and their families?

Similarly, Americans are losing faith in the companies that
are downsizing their jobs and paychecks. According to that
Chicago Tribune survey, 66 percent of Illinois voters denied
that "layoffs by big companies are really necessary so these
companies can stay competitive" and agreed that "these companies [are] only trying to make money."

The financier Felix Rohatyn has warned:

> The institutional relationship created by the mutual loyalty of
> employers and employees in most American businesses has
> been badly frayed [and] replaced by a combination of fear for
> the future and cynicism for the present as a broad proportion
> of working people see themselves as simply temporary assets
> to be hired or fired to "protect the bottom line" and "create
> shareholder value."

Working Americans feel the loss of loyalty. As a retired
laborer in Philadelphia said:

> There is no longer the relationship that once did exist between
> company and employee, where there was a bond, a family type

of feeling. Today, it's a "me" feeling: What's the bottom line? What am I going to get out of it? And we become expendable. I think that situation is ugly, not only for us as workers, but for us as a country.[25]

And a white-collar woman from Baltimore made much the same point:

I feel that it's a darn shame that people give so much of themselves and are so well educated that they still don't get the job security they should have. I don't know of anything more stressful than going to work not knowing if you're going back the next day. And having to pay your mortgage and your doctor bills and all that.[26]

In the aftermath of corporate downsizings, a sense of helplessness and bitterness fills not only those who have been fired but also those who remain on the job and must often work longer and harder than ever. David Noer, a vice president for the Center for Creative Leadership in Greensboro, North Carolina, estimates that some 75 percent of the Fortune 500 corporations have been affected by the "layoff-survivor syndrome." Sometimes, Noer says, workers take out their anger on company property, damaging computers or flattening tires. And, in ways that are less dramatic but just as painful, workplaces are becoming angrier and edgier, as people fear that their supervisors, their colleagues, and even their closest friends are plotting to preserve their jobs at others' expense.[27]

Amidst all this worry and rancor, Americans still yearn for the old-fashioned values of loyalty and community. The pervasiveness of this longing is reflected in the outpouring of admiration for two American heroes: the baseball player Cal Ripken, Jr., who is loyal to his fans and teammates, and the factory owner Aaron Feuerstein, who is loyal to his community and employees.

In September 1995, Americans honored Ripken — "the iron man" of the Baltimore Orioles — for his twelve-and-a-half-year streak of consecutive games played. At a time when professional ballplayers flit from team to team in response to multimillion-dollar offers, and team owners move their franchises from city to city to cash in on new opportunities, Ripken's loyalty to the Baltimore fans seemed even more admirable than an outstanding batting average or a home-run record. Significantly, Ripken was also notable for his loyalty to his fellow ball players. In August 1994, when the dispute between millionaire players and billionaire owners brought professional baseball to a halt, Ripken declared that he would honor his co-workers' picket lines if the owners tried to resume the season with strikebreakers. "If it's replacement players, it's not major league baseball, and I won't be playing," Ripken explained.

Later that month, Ripken told reporters that if the 1995 season began with replacement players, he would stay on strike, even at the risk of breaking his streak. Fortunately, the dispute was resolved in time for the 1995 season to begin. And the Orioles' owner, Peter Angelos, a former labor lawyer and a maverick among baseball's management figures, hesitated even to select replacement players last spring, partly for fear of placing Ripken in a difficult position.[28]

Three months later, Americans honored an employer who also exemplified the value of loyalty. Aaron Feuerstein owns a textile mill that his father had founded in the economically depressed community of Methuen, Massachusetts. Rather than move the plant south or overseas in search of cheap labor, Feuerstein modernized the product line, keeping the company profitable.

On the evening of December 11, while Feuerstein was enjoying a surprise seventieth birthday party, the plant was mostly destroyed by a flash fire. Paul Coorey, the president of Local 311 of the Union of Needletrades, Industrial, and Textile Employees, summed up how his co-workers felt as they watched the fire: "I was standing there, seeing the mill burn with my son, who also works there, and he looked at me and said, 'Dad, we just lost our jobs.' Years of our lives seemed gone." But rather than close the plant and throw twenty-four hundred employees out of work, Feuerstein rebuilt the factory and kept paying the workers. Hailed as a national hero, he said: "I haven't really done anything. I don't deserve credit. Corporate America has made it so that when you behave the way I did, it's abnormal."[29]

Restoring Community

When it's "abnormal" for a company to be loyal to its community, it's not surprising that Americans are losing confidence in large institutions and in one another. In a recent survey, conducted by Louis Harris and Associates for *Business Week,* fewer than 20 percent of all Americans expressed "a great deal of confidence" in any of these institutions: big business, the news media, congressional Republicans, congressional Democrats, Hollywood and the entertainment industry, state and local governments, labor unions, and the federal government.[30] Increasingly, people say the same thing I hear as I visit with working people around the country: "Nobody speaks for me."

At a time when anxiety is growing and confidence is declining, people are vulnerable to demagogues. Not surprisingly, working Americans have been listening to, and even voting for, voices like the talk-show host Rush Limbaugh and the presidential contender Pat Buchanan, who blame immigrants, minorities, and poor people for disappearing jobs and dwindling paychecks. My purpose in writing this book — and my goal for the AFL-CIO — is to help working Americans find their own voice and address their real problems. By building a new movement of working Americans, we can regain the strength to raise our living standards — and we can revive the spirit of confidence and community exemplified by Cal Ripken, Jr., Aaron Feuerstein, and countless unsung heroes. But before we can find our way out of our current predicament, we need to understand who got us into it — and how.

CHAPTER 3

Who's Doing It to You?

MOST AMERICANS understand that their living standards are declining, the gap between the rich and the rest of us is widening, and this inequality is tearing at the fabric of our society. What we need to know is: how did this happen? And who did it?

You've probably heard two very different explanations. The first story tells you that it's all the result of impersonal economic forces — global trade, new technologies, and the other trends that created what's called the new economy. The best thing to do is study more, work harder, and wait for things to work themselves out.

You hear this story from well-meaning, well-informed people — leading educators and economists, the most public-spirited corporate executives, the mainstream news media, and some prominent Democrats and Clinton administration officials. It's accurate as far as it goes, but it doesn't tell the whole story. And because it lacks passion and poetry, heroes and villains, I'd hate to have to defend it on a radio talk show — or in a bar-room argument.

The second account is more emotional and exciting. It gives us good guys and bad guys — mostly bad guys. The problem is that government got too big, took our tax money, and spent it on "them." "Them" is minorities, immigrants, government bureaucrats, greedy union members, or people with lax lifestyles promoted by Hollywood liberals. Usually, "them" is anyone the teller of the story doesn't like, anyone he or she thinks most Americans don't like — or anyone who isn't in the audience.[1]

You hear this story from the more mean-spirited business leaders, from most Republican campaigners at election time, all year round from talk-show hosts and right-wing demagogues like Limbaugh and Buchanan, and, at the farthest edge of extremism, from hate mongers like David Duke. It is important for every working American to know that the first story tells you just part of the truth — and the second story is a dangerous lie.

Yes, there is a new high-tech global economy. Working people saw it long ago, as factories moved overseas, imports flooded the stores, and our jobs were transformed by innovations from computer-assisted drafting in manufacturing companies to video-display terminals in most offices. In my years as a union representative, I saw the waves of changes wash over workers in industry after industry, from garment workers to elevator operators, janitors, health-care workers, and clerical workers, to name just a few. But the root cause of our problem is that corporate America decided to meet these challenges the wrong way. They didn't do it by building on America's traditional strengths: the know-how and love of experimentation that helped us develop the advanced technologies and the teamwork we displayed during World War II and the next three decades, when business, labor, and government worked together to help all Americans move forward. Instead, corporate America decided to break the postwar social contract — and to meet the challenge of global competition by wiping out jobs and driving down wages in pursuit of short-term profits.

The result: whatever gains have been made in competitiveness have come at a terrible price. Business has achieved its highest profitability in three decades, while most workers have seen their wages decline. We are on a "low-wage" path to noncompetitiveness. The decision to drive down living standards is at the root of many of the problems that make Americans believe our way of life is in jeopardy. With Americans working longer for less, our work ethic is challenged and our families are racked by the tensions of the "time famine." The greed and gaudiness of the wealthy, and the distorted values of the winner-take-all workplace, contribute to our sense that society is coming apart at the seams. And, as government serves the wealthy special interests, most people conclude that the political system is corrupt and broken.

I don't mean to put all the blame on just a few institutions. We all share some of the blame for letting corporate America drive down our living standards and distort our democratic process. For instance, we, the institution to which I've devoted my life — the labor movement — contributed to the crisis by letting our guard down. Too often, we failed to organize workers in the fastest-growing industries. Too often, we let our political efforts degenerate into mere financial contributions to glad-handing candidates. Too often, we kept our heads down, our minds closed, and our mouths shut during the great debates that shaped our nation's social and economic policies. Too often, we refused to reach out to potential allies who could have helped us build a coalition for challenging corporate priorities and offering positive alternatives.

That's why I'm making the case in this book — and devot-

ing my energies as president of the AFL-CIO — to reviving
the labor movement and building a new social movement that
will help Americans understand and solve our economic and
social problems. The weakness of labor and the absence of a
progressive social movement has created a dangerous vacuum
that's being filled by demagoguery and division.

Unless they are given a credible and compelling explanation
for what's gone wrong, good people facing hard times become vulnerable to opportunistic politicians who tell them
that the enemy is each other: racial and religious minorities,
immigrants and the poor, anyone who's different in any way —
"them, them, them." Growing social and racial antagonisms
injure innocent people, contribute to tensions in our communities, and worsen the sense that society is falling apart. Without a social movement that unites working people of all
colors and cultures, Americans will be powerless in the face of
falling living standards. And we will be in danger of fractur-
ing along the lines of race, ethnicity, religion, and lifestyle and
facing a future of more division, rancor, and violence.

I think back to one of the least attractive aspects of life
when I was growing up in the Bronx half a century ago.
Those weren't "the good old days" in every way, and one
reason was that there were certain neighborhoods where Jewish, Irish, or Italian kids — not to mention black or Puerto
Rican kids — knew they were unwelcome and unsafe. The
kids who would beat them up really weren't to blame; they
were acting on the enmity shown by their elders, the antago-
nism fueled by poverty and insecurity. That was bad enough
in the days when the worst you had to fear was a beating; it
got worse in the days of the switchblade. And it is tearing our
communities apart, now that children pack pistols and teenagers use automatic weapons.

Even people without prejudices seriously misunderstand the most important causes of stagnant living standards and social breakdown. In the recent Harris poll for *Business Week,* people were asked why "incomes for many working Americans have stayed flat for fifteen years." Seventy-three percent said "increased government spending [is a] major cause"; 61 percent blamed "high taxes"; 56 percent blamed "the decline of the manufacturing economy" (a good explanation, in my view); and 52 percent blamed "increasing global competition." But only 44 percent blamed "the excesses of big business and Wall Street," and just 24 percent listed "declining membership in labor unions" as a major cause of stagnant incomes.[2]

The most popular explanations tell only some — or none — of the story of falling incomes and a fractured society. Let's take a hard look at several of the partial or misleading explanations and find some real answers for who really did it. In this whodunit, we've got to sift the suspects, distinguishing among the entirely innocent, those who played a supporting role, and those who should shoulder the burden of the blame but have so far gotten away with the larceny of our living standards.

Is It Big Government?

So what about the most widely blamed scapegoats for stagnant living standards — big government and high taxes?

The problem isn't so much government's size as whom government serves. When it comes to helping working Americans, government is often too clumsy and costly. But when it comes to taking care of the wealthy and the well connected, government leaps into action with dazzling speed. That is why — especially since the Reagan tax revisions of the early 1980s — the tax code has been so heavily tilted in favor of the very wealthy and against working Americans.

Sorting through the tax changes of the 1980s and the late 1970s, one leading think tank found that they amounted to a tax cut averaging $45,565 for the top 1 percent of Americans. The next richest 4 percent got an average cut of $881. But the 60 percent of Americans who aren't very rich or very poor — the working middle class — had to pay several hundred dollars *more* per family because of increases in payroll taxes — not to mention increases in state and local taxes, as the federal government handed over many responsibilities to the states.[3]

To make things worse, the federal government ladles out special subsidies for big business — "corporate welfare," as it's come to be called. For instance, the federal tax system even encourages American companies to ship American jobs overseas. Here are two tax breaks that United States–based multinationals enjoy:

- Taking a credit against the corporate taxes for income taxes they pay to foreign countries, a tax break that costs the Treasury $25 billion a year.
- Deferring their income from their foreign operations, a tax break that costs $1.6 billion a year.

By the way, if you're looking for a president to blame for "big government" and high taxes, don't blame Bill Clinton. During the first three years of the Clinton administration, the federal workforce declined by 200,000 — mostly through attrition — making it the smallest since the presidency of John F. Kennedy.

And since Clinton became president, the only increase in federal income tax rates has been on the wealthiest 1 percent, while twenty million working families earning $28,500 a year or less actually got a tax credit. So the most recent changes in federal taxes are doing a little to reduce inequality and help working families make ends meet.

Is It "Them"?

Almost everyone's having a hard time in today's edgy workplaces. Some of those who are hurting the most are men in their forties and fifties — usually with family responsibilities — who expected to be reaching their prime earning years. Instead, they're up against the grim new realities of corporate downsizings and stagnant wages.

For instance, at a hearing the AFL-CIO conducted recently in Columbus, Ohio, a fifty-eight-year-old man named Dave Meyer told how he lost jobs as a middle manager at Rockwell International and McDonnell-Douglas after both companies relocated. Now, battling age discrimination, he can't find much more than jobs for $6 an hour.

Now Dave Meyer has no rancor toward anyone, but stories like his are why I can understand the fear and rage of the "angry white men," as well as the feelings of working men and women from every background who are caught in this economic squeeze. But the last thing working people need is to blame each other for their problems. That's why we should have no patience for those who tell white working men that the real problem is "them" — African Americans, Latinos, pushy working women, or whoever else is the scapegoat of the month. I try to tell this to white working men who are losing ground and looking for someone to blame: if "they" did it to you, how come "they" are doing even worse than you are?

African Americans still lag behind whites in job opportunities and pay levels. In 1994, the typical black worker earned $371 a week, just 80 percent of the median weekly wage of $467 for all workers. Hispanics earned even less — $354 a week, or only 70 percent of the median. Even though the education levels of black workers are rapidly achieving parity with white workers, African Americans' pay scales and job opportunities have been falling further behind whites' since 1980. If blacks are falling behind, how can they be benefiting significantly at the expense of whites?

As for women who work outside the home, they earn only seventy-two cents for every dollar men earn for year-round, full-time jobs. Anyhow, I doubt that any working person wants to hold down women's wages: nowadays, they're indispensable to most family budgets. If you're a working man whose wife is also working outside the home, your family benefits from policies that prohibit corporate America from discriminating against women in pay and promotions. And if, like me, you're the father of a young woman just beginning her career, I'm sure you want her to be able to go as far as her talents can take her, and not be held back by prejudice or kept down by glass ceilings.

So, are long-overdue efforts against discrimination by race or sex — including the varied programs that go under the label affirmative action — really to blame for the decline in workers' wages? Not likely. For all the argument about affirmative action, consider this: could it possibly have influenced forty-three million employment decisions over the past sixteen years? That's how many jobs were eliminated by corporate downsizings. And has affirmative action influenced what happened to 75,000 jobs — or even 50,000 or 40,000? That's how many jobs have been wiped out at General Motors, Sears, Roebuck, and AT&T (as originally announced) — and in pursuit of corporate profits, not of social justice.

While we're at it, what about welfare recipients? As it happens, many of the stereotypes are not entirely right: 38 percent of the families receiving Aid to Families with Dependent Children are non-Hispanic white; 39 percent are black; 17 percent are Hispanic; and 3 percent are Asian Americans. And AFDC accounts for less than 1 percent of your federal tax dollars. Welfare is a symptom of the tangle of social problems — from teenage pregnancies to family breakups. And it's a symptom of economic problems as well, including the fact that too many low-wage jobs pay less than public assistance. But it isn't the reason why working people's paychecks aren't growing.

In today's economy, I can understand why there are "angry white men." But let's direct our anger at those who deserve it — the folks in the executive suites who are cutting wages and slashing jobs, and the politicians who provide them with corporate welfare and tax windfalls.

Is It Low Skills?

From 1973 through 1993, the hourly wages of high school graduates and high school dropouts fell by 14.7 percent and 22.5 percent, respectively. Meanwhile, during the 1980s, college-educated workers actually increased their real hourly pay. And those with more than two years of education past a baccalaureate degree saw their hourly earnings grow by more than 8 percent.

These facts fed an easy explanation for falling wages and

increasing inequality: in the new economy, if you've got education, training, and skills, you're doing just fine. But if you're an "unskilled worker" — and, for too many of our nation's leaders, that means anyone without a four-year college degree — you'd better accept the fact that soon the economy won't offer you a secure and good-paying job.

That explanation isn't entirely wrong, and those who offer it often have the best intentions. Yes, it's true that new technology and worldwide trade place a premium on specialized skills and the ability to learn new ones. And America should do everything it can to offer everyone, young and old, all the schooling and training they need. That is why my old local union, which represents building service workers in New York City, offers a training program to teach the members new skills for new jobs — and why we offer college scholarships to help the members' kids go to college. And that is why I, for one, give Bill Clinton high marks for everything he's doing to expand educational opportunities: raising standards in the public schools, helping kids who aren't going on to college learn job skills, providing low-cost college loans for young people from working-class families, and improving job-training programs for mature workers who need new jobs or better jobs. My parents raised me to love learning, and in my book, you can't do enough to offer people schooling and skill training.

But it's simplistic to suggest that falling wages can be explained by "low skills" or that expanding inequality is caused by an "education premium." For one thing, it's not only arrogant but wrongheaded to call 75 percent of American workers "unskilled" just because they don't have four-year college degrees. Some of the highest-skilled workers I've ever met — from cutters in the garment industry, like the late union leader David Dubinsky, to licensed electricians, chefs like my son John is studying to become, and a number of young computer geniuses — either never finished or never went to college.

And I don't mind telling you that a number of the most foolish people I've ever met — sometimes sitting across from me at the bargaining table — hold advanced degrees from some of the finest universities. Here, I think a worker in a dietary unit in a hospital in Somerville, Massachusetts, may have said it best. Complaining about her young supervisor, she said contemptuously, "All he has is college knowledge." We've got to distinguish between skills and credentials, and find ways to continue to train, honor, and reward people who can do important things and do them well, even if their crafts aren't taught in college.

Anyhow, since 1987, college-educated people, as well as those without four-year degrees, also have seen their incomes stagnate. From 1989 through 1993, the real wages of college graduates fell 1.2 percent, and the earnings of those with postgraduate education fell 2.1 percent. All this suggests that, even for the college-educated, incomes are subject to the law of economic gravity. The shrinking of middle management and the shakeouts in several white-collar industries — banking, finance, insurance, real estate, and computers — all are dragging down college-educated Americans, right along with the rest of the workforce.

Similarly, paycheck realities suggest that college-educated workers, like all other workers, benefit from having some form of power when dealing with their employers. In my years in the labor movement, I've seen how college-educated professionals such as teachers, social workers, and newspaper reporters have raised their incomes by organizing unions and bargaining with their employers, while others, such as doctors, benefit from associations that virtually control their professions. And I've also seen how other skilled, educated professionals find their earnings languish because they have little leverage over their employers and industries. So, of course, we need to do everything we can to provide the education and training for everyone to participate in the new economy.

But let's face the facts: most workers aren't losing out because they aren't sufficiently skilled. In fact, American workers are the best educated in the world. And even the best educated and most skilled are subject to national economic trends — and they'd do well to join with other working Americans to get incomes moving up again.

Is It Technology?

For those who explain stagnant wages and increasing inequality by pointing to a mismatch between workers' skills and job requirements, technology is a big piece of the puzzle. But does technology automatically drag down wages for most workers? Or is the real problem how employers use technology?

For all the innovation in the past two decades, this hasn't been the only era in our history when technology advanced. Earlier in this century, the internal combustion engine, the assembly line, and advances in aeronautics all raised wages and living standards for working Americans. One reason for these gains was that working people joined together, at the workplace and in politics, to make sure that they shared in the gains of growing progress and prosperity. Now, the question is whether corporate America will use advances in communications, transportation, and computerized information to enable working people to gain more skills, more discretion on the job, and increased living standards.

So far, most corporations have used new technologies to increase their own power and profits, not the workers' participation and paychecks. New technology makes plants, equipment, and investment capital more mobile, giving managers more power to move production to low-wage areas overseas. And, in this country, management is using technology to transfer judgment and decision making from workers to supervisors, eliminating some jobs and cutting wages for others. Often, employees — particularly office workers — find their every action monitored by computerized information systems, which threaten their personal privacy and human dignity. For too many workers — white collar, blue collar, and "new collar" — the high-tech workplace is a stressful cybernetic sweatshop.

It doesn't have to be this way. Unions are fighting to train workers to use new technologies and to gain their autonomy and discretion on the job. Far from being an impersonal force that inevitably drives down workers' wages and destroys human dignity, technology is like any tool: what matters most is how people use it.

Is It the Global Economy?

More than technology, unrestricted global trade is a force that does tend to drive down wages in advanced countries. In the labor analyst Richard Rothstein's memorable phrase, trade plunges American workers into "the global hiring hall," where they are forced to compete with workers in low-wage countries around the world that often permit child labor and lack minimum-wage laws and other basic labor protections.

In China, for instance, girls as young as ten work fourteen-hour days for as little as $10 a month. In Bangladesh, children younger than thirteen are paid $7.50 a month and often work twenty hours a day. And in Malaysia, the world's largest exporter of semiconductors, electronics workers make forty-five cents an hour.[4]

Although every advanced industrialized nation is part of the global economy, the United States is experiencing the most extreme declines in wages and increases in inequality. In the United States, hourly compensation — wages and benefits — for manufacturing and production workers fell by 0.6 percent a year between 1979 and 1989. During the same period, hourly compensation grew by 1.3 percent a year in Japan, 1.9 percent in Germany, and 1.9 percent in France. In fact, compared with pay scales in the United States, wages for industrial workers are 25 percent higher in Japan and 60 percent higher in Germany.

But while American companies (and copy-cat foreign companies doing business in the United States) sought a competitive edge by driving down wages, they also raised prices, dividend payments, and executive salaries. These moves heightened the inequality in wages and wealth far more rapidly in the United States than in any other advanced industrial nation. Globalization is being accompanied by problems in this country that aren't happening anywhere else on the globe. That suggests that, as with technology, the problem isn't the challenge of global competition; it is how our economy is responding to it.

Part of the problem is United States trade policies that put American workers at a disadvantage against other countries that discriminate against our products. Our merchandise trade deficit jumped to $151 billion in 1994, and it's expected to exceed $185 billion for 1995. Using the estimate that each $1 billion of the trade deficit destroys 17,000 U.S. jobs, the $151 billion deficit wiped out 2,570,000 jobs just in 1994.

But much of the competition American workers face has its origins right here in the United States. American-based multinational corporations have invested $612 billion abroad, especially in low-wage areas of Asia and Latin America. In 1994 alone, new United States investment totaled $58.5 billion, increasing by 17 percent in Asia and the Pacific and 14 percent in Latin America. These holdings produce goods for export to advanced industrial nations, including the United States. So when it comes to foreign competition that is destroying our jobs, American workers can echo the famous cartoon character Pogo: "We have met the enemy, and he is us." Or, more accurately, we have met the enemies, and they are American-based multinational corporations. The problem isn't their pursuit of overseas investment opportunities; the problem is their pursuit of cheap labor — and the failure of American government and business to insist on minimal standards and decency in the treatment of workers overseas.

All this confirms the conclusion of this whodunit. Stagnant wages weren't caused by big government, minorities, and the poor, or by a "skills mismatch." The problem isn't even the challenge of the high-tech global economy. The problem is how corporate America has decided to meet the challenge.

Taking the Low-Wage Path

The early 1970s were a turning point for corporate America. Up against new difficulties, they decided to break their post-war social contract with working America and compete in the global economy by driving down wages. After a quarter-century when the United States dominated the world economy, the 1970s brought unexpected challenges. As Western European and Japanese manufacturers grew stronger, the United States ran a trade deficit in 1971 — the first since 1893. Japanese producers, in particular, gained on American companies in worldwide and even American markets in important industries, including autos, steel, semiconductors, and electronics. In the automobile industry alone, between 1973 and 1982, U.S. companies lost 16 percent of the U.S. auto market to the Japanese. And, as American auto companies lost sales, cut back production, and laid off workers, the shock waves hit other American industries, including steel, rubber, and the service sector.

Corporate America's woes were worsened by the oil embargoes of 1973 and 1979. These "oil shocks" boosted energy costs and increased the competitive advantage of Japanese and German auto companies, which enjoyed a head start in building inexpensive, energy-efficient small cars. The failure of American auto companies to take the lead in building small cars offers a practical example of the need to involve workers and their unions in decision making. Years before the energy crisis of the 1970s, the visionary president of the United Auto Workers, Walter Reuther, saw the success of the German-made Volkswagen "bug" and urged United States auto companies to develop high-quality small cars. After the auto companies rejected his concept as unprofitable, Reuther proposed that General Motors, Ford, and Chrysler be exempted from antitrust legislation so that they could develop an American small car as a joint project, with one company building the body, another the transaxle, and another the engine. But the nation's political and economic elites didn't listen to Reuther, and decades later, American workers suffered for their employers' shortsightedness.[5]

So corporate America faced the costs of a crisis largely of its own making. Instead of cooperating with workers and improving the quality of goods and services, most business leaders decided to compete in the global marketplace by driving down American wages and living standards. Starting in the 1970s, corporate America took a more aggressive stance with workers — union and nonunion alike. Corporations started resisting wage increases for unionized employees, fighting organizing efforts by nonunion employees, and even driving unions out of unionized workplaces. In the automobile, rubber, and electronics industries, companies with thirty years or more of stable collective-bargaining relationships closed down high-wage, unionized operations in the Northeast and Midwest and opened up nonunion, low-wage operations in the South and Southwest.

Corporate America became the most formidable force in the legislative arena. In 1972, corporate chief executive officers founded a new national lobbying organization, the Business Roundtable. In 1978, the Roundtable defeated proposals to reform the nation's labor laws so that it would be more difficult for employers to intimidate workers who were organizing unions. The Business Roundtable dramatized its growing power when it flew a platoon of business leaders to Washington in a flotilla of corporate jets to lobby Congress against labor-law reform. Then, emboldened by this victory, business pursued an ambitious agenda — deregulating energy, finance, and transportation, cutting taxes for wealthy investors, and weakening wage protections for workers in construction and other industries.

Meanwhile, big business strengthened its political clout, making election campaigns depend more on money and less on people. From the mid-1970s to 1987, the number of corporate political action committees increased from 89 to 1816, and their war chests grew from $8 million to $96.9 million.[6]

Looking back on the 1970s, the journalist Thomas Edsall wrote:

> During the 1970s, business refined its ability to act as a class, submerging competitive instincts in favor of joint, cooperative action in the legislative arena. Rather than individual companies seeking only special favor in the reward of a contract, in the dropping of an antitrust case, or in State Department assistance in gaining exclusive franchising rights in a foreign country, the dominant theme in the political strategy of business became a shared interest in the defeat of bills such as consumer protection and labor law reform.[7]

Just as important as victories by business on substantive issues was the sense that employers had abandoned the shared understandings that guided America during the postwar era. As the president of the UAW, Douglas Fraser, declared in 1978, when he resigned from a joint labor-management committee on national economic policy, "The leaders of industry, commerce, and finance in the United States have broken and discarded the fragile, unwritten compact previously existing during a period of growth and progress."[8]

During the 1980s, business and government did even more to break faith with working Americans. The Reagan and

Bush administrations pursued policies that destroyed jobs, drove down wages, and strengthened employers at the expense of employees. And from the 1980s through the 1990s, corporate America continued to downsize its workforce and their wages. The strategy worked — for the fortunate few. The incomes of the wealthiest 1 percent grew even more quickly in the 1980s than in the golden era of the 1950s and 1960s. In 1994 and 1995, corporate America earned the highest after-tax profits in thirty years. But while they achieved their goal, working families did not raise their living standards.

Washington's War on Workers

From 1981 through 1992, the Reagan and Bush administrations took America further down the low-wage path. National policies dampened the growth of employment, encouraged corporate mergers and downsizings, sent jobs overseas, held down the minimum wage, and strengthened employers at the expense of their employees.

Dampening Growth

Workers have a hard time getting raises when the economy is sluggish. During the 1980s, the Federal Reserve Board held down growth in production, jobs, and wages in the interest of fighting inflation. As the Congressional Democratic Policy Committee reported:

> Any careful reading of the minutes of the Fed's Open Market Committee will reveal that decisions on interest rate policy since the mid-1980s have been principally driven by whether

or not the economy had sufficient momentum to allow workers to stiffen wage demands. At the point at which such momentum appeared (or was even suspected), the Fed has tightened monetary policy, pushing up the cost of monthly mortgage payments and car loans to the point that the level of construction and manufacturing subsided and workers refocused on the question of keeping jobs, rather than improving pay.[9]

Motivating Merger Mania

During the 1980s, companies swallowed each other up with borrowed money. Just to pay off the junk bonds and the interest on these leveraged buyouts, the executives who survived the corporate feeding frenzy frequently wiped out workers' jobs or cut their wages. This trend was actually encouraged by the Reagan administration, with Assistant Attorney General William Baxter's "open season" for corporate mergers and acquisitions. And the University of California law professor David Vogel noted that the Reagan administration also encouraged "merger mania" by weakening the antitrust authority of the Federal Trade Commission and Interstate Commerce Commission.

Exporting American Jobs

In the early 1980s, as the United States borrowed money overseas to finance the burgeoning federal budget deficit, the dollar became more and more overvalued. This made American products more expensive on the world market, thereby reducing our exports, increasing our imports, and encouraging U.S. companies to move production overseas. The trends cost American jobs and also contributed to a climate in which American wages were frozen or even cut.

Making the Minimum Wage a Poverty Wage

The minimum wage was frozen from 1981 through 1989, its purchasing power reduced by 16 percent. In fact, the last time the minimum wage allowed a family of three to live above the poverty line was in 1980.

Freezing the minimum wage for a decade contributed to the growth in the numbers of the working poor to more than twelve million Americans. And it also held down earnings for employees in industries that often pay nonunion workers just a little above the minimum wage: clothing and textiles, hotels and restaurants, hospitals and health care, and building service and maintenance. The erosion of the minimum wage has dragged down the wages of the lowest-paid 20 percent of the workforce. Most of these workers aren't well-to-do suburban teenagers; they're usually adult working women whose wages are essential for their families.

Strengthening Management's Hand

In addition to creating an economic environment in which employers call all the shots, the Reagan and Bush administrations pursued policies that specifically strengthened corporate managers against their employees.

When Reagan broke the air traffic controllers' strike in 1981 by permanently replacing the strikers, he set an example for corporate America. Soon, major corporations were breaking a taboo that had existed since the passage of the National Labor Relations Act in 1935; they used strikebreakers as permanent replacements for striking workers. This further tilted the balance of power against working Americans and helped drive down wages. Also, Presidents Reagan and Bush appointed members of the National Labor Relations Board — the referee between labor and management — who tilted toward employers on most major issues. The NLRB-packing began in 1981, when Reagan selected as its chairman John Van de Water, a UCLA law professor who had served as a management consultant in 130 union representation elections. He boasted that he had helped management win 125 of them.[10]

Finally, the Carter, Reagan, and Bush administrations all weakened workers by deregulating major industries, including rail, airlines, trucking, and interstate bus lines. These moves had the effect of upsetting national labor contracts, weakening unions, and driving down wages.

Corporate America's Attack

Emboldened by friendly administrations, corporate America spent the 1980s continuing to cut wages and jobs — trends that have continued well into the present decade. The corporate offensive included relocating plants and facilities to low-wage areas in America and around the world, contracting out operations to low-wage companies, and breaking existing unions and blocking organizing drives. These tactics have been encouraged by Wall Street and financial markets, which favor short-term profit taking over long-term strategies for growth.

Runaway Shops Go Global

Just as companies spent the 1960s and 1970s searching for low-wage labor here at home, they spent the 1980s and early 1990s searching for low-wage labor abroad. United States–

based businesses are shedding their American identities to become self-styled citizens of the world. Their attitude was exemplified by Gilbert Williamson, president of the NCR Corporation, who declared in 1989: "I was asked the other day about United States competitiveness, and I replied that I don't think about it at all. We at NCR think of ourselves as a globally competitive company that happens to be headquartered in the United States."[11] (NCR had grown and prospered as National Cash Register, rooted and headquartered in Dayton, Ohio. Ironically, the "globally competitive" NCR was swallowed up and later spat out by AT&T.)

Multinational corporations that "happen to be headquartered in the United States" invested abroad at a record rate in 1994; their overseas holdings increased to $612 billion. They poured the most money into low-wage areas in Asia and Latin America; there, United States investment increased by 17 percent and 14 percent, respectively, during 1994.

Expanding abroad often leads to downsizing at home. For instance, AT&T has increased its overseas workforce by sixty thousand over the past decade. At the same time, it has eliminated some hundred thousand jobs here in the United States.

Cutting Wages by Outsourcing

Another wage-cutting tactic is replacing in-house operations with outside contractors. Often, the in-house workers are union and high wage, while the outside companies are nonunion and low wage.

Among the major companies using this strategy is General Motors, whose insistence on outsourcing the production of auto parts caused a bitter and costly strike in March 1996. Mobil is planning to lay off most of its clerical and support staff and subcontract the work to lower-paying outside companies. State and local governments are privatizing public services to replace higher-paid public employees with lower-paid employees of private contractors. And, in addition to GM, other corporations have downsizing plans that are a cause of a growing number of labor disputes, from the strike at Boeing to the drawn-out contract negotiations at Bell Atlantic.[12]

Waging War on Labor

Encouraged by President Reagan's firing of the striking air traffic controllers, major companies, including Greyhound, Phelps Dodge, and Eastern Airlines, also used permanent replacement workers to break strikes. This tactic discouraged strikes and further tilted the balance of power against labor. In 1995, there were only thirty-two strikes involving a thousand workers or more — compared with eight times as many strikes on that scale in 1975.

Writing in *The New Republic,* the journalist John Judis showed how the war on workers drove down wages for employees — union and nonunion — in major industries. Steelworkers' wages declined from $20.37 an hour in 1981 to $16.87 an hour in 1992 (all figures in 1992 dollars). Meatpacking workers' wages dropped from $13.98 to $9.15 an hour during that period. And restaurant workers' wages fell from $6.14 to $5.29.[13]

And Wall Street Cheered

All these cuts in jobs and wages were applauded by Wall Street and the financial markets. While workforces and pay scales have been downsized, the thirty companies that make up the Dow Jones Industrial Average have seen their share prices increase by more than 200 percent over the past ten years. All this suggests that Wall Street favors cutting labor costs as a strategy for boosting profits, rather than patient, long-term efforts to sharpen workers' skills, improve the quality of goods and services, and expand markets and sales. And because so many top executives hold large shares of corporate stock, with options to buy more, they have a vested interest in making decisions to lay off workers and hold down wages, thereby increasing the value of their own portfolios.

What's Wrong with These Pictures?

Corporate America's relentless drive to cut labor costs — and Wall Street's cheering on the effort — explained some of the sad stories that made headlines in 1995 and some crises I inherited when I became president of the AFL-CIO.

Chase Manhattan and Chemical Bank announced a merger that put twelve thousand people out of work. Their stock soared. The agricultural equipment manufacturer Caterpillar was enjoying improving productivity and racking up record profits. Then it installed a two-tier wage system (where newly hired workers are paid less than long-time employees for the same jobs), scheduled work on weekends without paying overtime, and rejected the traditional system of industry-wide collective bargaining. It forced thousands of workers on strike, committed three hundred unfair labor practices — and racked up more record profits.

And Arizona and the city of Phoenix bailed America West Airlines out of bankruptcy, with tax breaks and revenue bonds. The airline promised workers it would not contract out hangar jobs, and it rebounded with eleven straight quarters of profitability and stacked up $300 million in reserves. Then the Teamsters started an organizing drive for machinists at America West. The company thumbed its nose at the community by firing 396 $35,000-a-year mechanics and contracting out their jobs to a company in Everett, Washington, where mechanics make only $21,000.

When I tell that story, I like to ask my audiences — especially if they're business people who fly frequently — "How many of you want to fly in an airplane that's just been repaired by a $21,000-a-year rookie mechanic?" Not too many people raise their hands.

Now, the America West story has a happy ending. In an election conducted by the National Mediation Board in April 1996, the company's mechanics voted by 587 to 135 to be represented by the Teamsters. Stories like these explain why a shrewd Wall Street analyst, Stephen Roach, the chief economist at Morgan Stanley, says that business is carving itself a disproportionate slice of a pie that's supposed to be shared with workers. And he warns that employers will face a "backlash" unless workers "begin to receive a just reward."

Silencing Working People's Voices

Corporate America's war on workers has stifled the spirit of our national labor laws. Since it was passed, in 1935, the National Labor Relations Act has promised working people the right to organize unions and to bargain with their employers — all without fear of being fired for union activity. Now, because of corporate America's hostility and official Washington's indifference, that promise of industrial democracy has been broken.

As part of the attack on working Americans that began during the 1970s, corporate America stepped up its efforts to prevent employees from organizing unions. Associations of employers offered extensive union-busting services to their member companies. Leading the way, the National Association of Manufacturers created the Council on a Union-Free Environment. A new class of professionals emerged: lawyers, management consultants, and industrial psychologists all primed to help companies defeat organizing campaigns, drive unions out of their workplaces, and drag out contract negotiations to the point where workers would settle for cuts in pay and benefits. By the early 1990s, there were more than fifteen hundred consultants earning $500 million a year advising employers on how to defeat organizing campaigns.[14] With enormous resources and expert help, corporations were able to exploit every loophole in labor law, thus making a mockery of the election process administered by the National Labor Relations Board.

Here's how the system is supposed to work — and here's what really happens most of the time:[15]

1. Employees in a company in an "appropriate unit" — production workers in a factory, nurses in a hospital, clerical employees in an office — sign cards authorizing a union to bargain with management over their wages, benefits, and working conditions.

2. If a majority of the workers sign, the union can ask the company to begin contract negotiations.

3. Usually, the company refuses to recognize the union. In that case, the union asks the National Labor Relations Board to conduct a secret-ballot election in the bargaining unit.

4. Then comes the campaign. Employers are free to bombard workers with anti-union messages, often with the help of high-priced lawyers, communications consultants, and industrial psychologists. Everything about the company and its campaign emphasizes its overwhelming power over the employees.

Often, employers fire leading union supporters in violation of the law — and wait for years until the NLRB or the courts order them to reinstate these workers. The Harvard law professor Paul Weiler has estimated that some ten thousand workers — one in twenty of all those supporting organizing campaigns — are fired each year, simply for trying to bring unions into their workplaces.[16]

The union, on the other hand, seems limited to the brave members of the workers' organizing committee and a handful of full-time staff who do not have the opportunity, as the employers do, to meet with workers individually or in groups during working hours.

5. As one organizer has observed, "The campaign is conducted and won or lost on the narrow issue of which is more credible — the union's promises or the company's threats."[17] It's a tribute to the courage of working Americans that unions win about half of all NLRB elections.

6. If the union wins, the battle still isn't over. Often, the company will challenge the election result, sometimes dragging out the process for years and delaying contract negotiations. By way of comparison, imagine if Bill Clinton hadn't been able to take office in January 1993 — or even in January 1995 — because George Bush was still challenging the results of the 1992 presidential election. Here, too, when management gets away with refusing to bargain even after the workers win an election, it sends the message that the com-

pany is overwhelmingly powerful and the union is inherently weak.

7. If the company accepts a union victory in the election, it must bargain with the union "in good faith." Often, the company refuses to bargain in good faith — sometimes demanding cuts in pay and benefits — so management and the union reach an impasse. The company can then unilaterally put its final proposal into effect — or "lock out" the workers until they accept it. And the union can strike. Even though the company cannot legally fire strikers, it can "permanently replace" them, a distinction without a difference. Because the NLRB election process is now so heavily tilted in favor of management, the entire experience — far from empowering workers — can be a hellish ordeal for many of them.

In testimony before a presidential commission on labor law, department store employee Judy Ray told how her company harassed and eventually fired her because she had supported a union organizing effort:

> I was a ten-year employee of Jordan Marsh, in Peabody [Massachusetts], up until this day after Thanksgiving, on which I was fired. I was fired, I truly believe, solely because I was a union organizer within the store. . . .
>
> I cannot impress on you . . . what an employee who is just fighting for their rights in a campaign goes through this day and age. I have been followed on my day off, to restaurants, by security guards with walkie-talkies. I had an employee, a management person, assigned to work with me eight hours a day, five days a week, who was told he was there solely to work on me, to change my ideas about unions.
>
> I was timed going to the bathroom. I could go nowhere in my workplace without being followed.[18]

Similarly, companies stepped up their efforts to get rid of existing unions. Florence Hill, a worker at Highland Yarn Mills and the wife of the local union president, told the presidential commission:

> I was not allowed off my little section that I worked in. When I'd go to the bathroom, my supervisor would follow me. Anywheres I went, I was being followed. I'd go take my break; they'd cut me down to two ten-minute breaks and a fifteen-minute break. . . .
>
> I'd go through the mill. I'd always been a happy-go-lucky person, I would speak and I — you know, be friendly with people. But I got, as time — I'd have to hold my head down when I walked because I didn't know what I was going to see, I didn't know what these people were going to do to me. . . .
>
> And then the stress got so bad that I did have a heart attack. But when I came back, they didn't let up on me. . . . And my supervisor made the remark that he didn't know how I had been taking what I had been taking without walking out the door or dropping over dead.
>
> That was what they were waiting for, for me to drop over dead.[19]

Creating a New Voice for Working Americans

Of course, business and government shouldn't shoulder all the blame for the decline in working people's living standards. We in the labor movement are also partly at fault because, over the past few decades, we let our guard down. Too many unions became complacent, and the best evidence of that is the decline in labor's organizing effort.

In 1950, unions initiated more than 5600 representation

elections, offering almost 900,000 working people the opportunity to have a voice in their workplaces. By 1970, labor sought more elections — over eight thousand in all — but unions were seeking smaller units. So the number of workers who had the opportunity to vote for union representation declined to 545,000. By 1990, the decline in organizing activity was unmistakable: unions filed for only 3628 elections covering only 230,000 workers.

Not surprisingly, we ended up organizing fewer workers. Early in the 1950s, unions successfully organized an average of a half million workers a year. By the end of the 1980s, we were organizing only about eighty thousand workers in private industry each year — far fewer than the number of union members who lost their jobs in mass layoffs.

To be sure, the shortcomings of the law and the hostility of management made it harder than ever to organize workers. But the tragedy was that too many unions seemed simply to have stopped trying at all. At every level, by the beginning of the 1990s, the entire labor movement was spending less than 5 percent of its resources — just one dollar out of every twenty — on organizing. Unions spent most of their resources on representing current members at the bargaining table, in grievances and arbitrations, and in the political and legislative process. In short, they spent 95 percent of their resources on the 15 percent of workers who were already organized and only 5 percent on the 85 percent who were not organized.

This may have made sense when unions represented a third of all American workers. But by the beginning of the 1990s, we had found that the structures and strategies that succeeded during very different times were no longer effective, since the source of strength — our membership — had declined to fewer than one in six workers.

In many industries, we were rapidly losing the strength to represent our members effectively — from the bargaining tables to the halls of Congress. Yes, it was still true that union members earn much more than nonunion workers. In fact, with the beating nonunion workers were taking, the "union premium" in wages and benefits has grown from between 10 and 15 percent during the 1960s to more than 20 percent today. But even our greatest accomplishments became an incitement for employers to try to destroy existing unions, defeat organizing drives, or compete against unionized companies by taking the low road of low wages.

The decline in organizing also meant that unions had virtually stopped conducting a dialogue with working Americans outside our ranks. One of many reasons that organizing is an essential element of unionism is that it keeps us abreast with the aspirations, attitudes, and conditions of working people beyond our own workplaces — information that's essential for us in representing our own members as well as in expanding our membership base. And, while too many unions failed to conduct a dialogue with working Americans, too many working Americans had stopped thinking about unions at all — or dismissed us as dinosaurs. In a survey the AFL-CIO itself commissioned in 1993, most nonunion workers said unions were "not an important part of how they see the world." In discussion groups, participants said they had problems on their jobs, but "it literally did not occur to them to look to unions as a solution."[20]

By the beginning of the 1990s, more and more union people understood that we had to change our ways, starting with a renewed commitment to organizing. For one thing, many union activists became convinced that the only way to protect the living standards of union members was to be sure that every worker making similar products or providing similar services receives decent wages and benefits. Only then would we have the power to make sure that companies compete by improving quality, not by lowering wages and benefits.

Of course, many unions were making extraordinary efforts at organizing, including some in such basic industries as clothing and textiles, which were hemorrhaging jobs. In response to the management hostility and government indifference, union activists began to develop new ways of organizing to build working people's power in a workplace, a company, a community, or an entire industry. Whether or not the union eventually petitioned for an election supervised by the NLRB, the purpose of these campaigns was to build working people's leverage over management, so that they could convince employers to recognize their union and improve their pay and conditions.

Many of these techniques were taught and refined at the AFL-CIO Organizing Institute, a center that was created outside the labor center's Washington headquarters, with early support from the federation and some of the most activist unions, including AFSCME, the Amalgamated Clothing and Textile Workers, the Carpenters, SEIU, the Steelworkers, and the United Food and Commercial Workers. Soon, many unions were relying on the institute for advice on organizing strategy. And as the institute graduated a larger number of organizers each year — from recent college graduates to rank-and-file union members — unions hired them and were eager for more.

A New Voice for Working People

As union activists searched for better ways to organize and represent working people, they took a hard look at every level of the labor movement — from their local unions to the national labor center, the AFL-CIO.

Founded in 1955 as a result of the merger of the craft unions of the American Federation of Labor and the industry-wide unions of the Congress of Industrial Organizations, the AFL-CIO should speak for American workers. During the 1950s and 1960s, under the leadership of the legendary cigar-smoking patriarch George Meany, the AFL-CIO was one of the most prominent participants in national affairs. Meany was a master at wielding power, and, under his leadership, the AFL-CIO used its power for the good of working Americans well beyond its ranks. Civil rights, voting rights, Medicare, Medicaid, and programs for housing and education — all were pushed to passage with the help of the AFL-CIO under the leadership of Meany and other strong leaders, such as Walter Reuther of the United Auto Workers and the civil rights advocate A. Philip Randolph of the Brotherhood of Sleeping Car Porters.

Yet, while the AFL-CIO was brilliantly effective at using its power, even then it was losing sight of the need to maintain and build its power. This shortcoming became more apparent in the 1980s and 1990s, after Meany passed from the scene and labor's share of the workforce dramatically declined, and with it our bargaining power, political clout, and media visibility.

I will always believe that Meany's successor, Lane Kirkland, earned an honorable place in history. Certainly, he took office at a difficult time, just before the beginning of the Reagan-Bush era and a decade of massive layoffs in manufacturing. Particularly in his early years as president, Kirkland did his best to lead a revival of the labor movement. He negotiated the return of the United Auto Workers, the United Mine Workers, and the Teamsters to the AFL-CIO. He led the Solidarity Day mobilization of union members in Washington, D.C., to protest the Reagan administration's attacks on working people. And he changed the course of world history with his support of the Solidarity trade union in Poland, a movement that contributed to the fall of communism in Eastern Europe and the Soviet Union.

In particular, Kirkland's deputy, my old friend Tom Donahue, was an easygoing but effective innovator. Tom initiated and led an AFL-CIO committee on the future of work, which frankly acknowledged that the labor movement had fallen behind the pace of change, and called for experiments, such as offering services to "associate members" who are interested in unions but are not covered under union contracts — anyone from union members who have been laid off from their jobs to employees in nonunion workplaces who are interested in organizing. Tom was a supporter of the AFL-CIO's Organizing Institute at a time when many in labor's hierarchy were skeptical of the energetic young organizers it recruited and trained. And he also was a pioneer in expanding labor's communications efforts, building a TV studio at the AFL-CIO headquarters.

Yet, for all its good intentions and good work, the AFL-CIO seemed increasingly removed from the daily struggles of American workers. While Meany's AFL-CIO had brandished power, the AFL-CIO of the 1980s and early 1990s too often seemed content to generate position papers — thoughtful ones, to be sure, but with little effect on workers' lives beyond the Washington Beltway. Indeed, surveys showed that fewer than 5 percent of union members — much less workers outside our ranks — had even heard of the scholarly Kirkland, who avoided appearances on national television. In their times, Meany, Reuther, Randolph, Hillman, Dubinsky, Quill, and John L. Lewis had all been visible and vocal in the news media; many of us yearned for a strong voice and a visible presence in the debates of the 1990s.

For the leaders of many of the fastest-growing unions, our dissatisfaction with the federation's headquarters grew deeper during 1993 and 1994. With Bill Clinton's election in 1992, we had, for the first time in twelve years, a president who was not our sworn enemy. Yet labor continued to lose almost as many legislative battles in Washington as we won: failing to defeat the North American Free Trade Agreement, to enact a ban on permanent replacements of striking workers, or to move meaningful labor law reforms through a blue-ribbon presidential commission and onto the floor of Congress.

Our sense of alarm increased with the November 1994 elections, when Republicans, intent on repealing sixty years of social progress, captured control of both houses of Congress. Working Americans had come to a critical point — with corporations downsizing, wages stagnating, unions declining, and our enemies seizing control of Congress. We waited for the top leader of the AFL-CIO to raise his voice or sound his trumpet — but the silence was deafening.

As much as anyone, it was the tough, gruff president of AFSCME, Gerald McEntee, who forced the issue that it was time for Kirkland, who was seventy-three and had served for sixteen years, to retire or be replaced. At the February meeting of the AFL-CIO executive council, a coalition called for

Kirkland's retirement and, more important, for a reexamination and revitalization of the federation's programs. We hoped that Donahue would challenge Kirkland, but Donahue declined, expressing his loyalty to Kirkland and his own intention to retire. What followed was the first contested election in the history of the AFL-CIO. I was nominated for president by the unions that had challenged Kirkland, a remarkable coalition that included my home union, the Service Employees; the federation's largest union, the Teamsters; the public employee union AFSCME; leading industrial unions, such as the UAW, Steelworkers, Machinists, Mine Workers, Rubber Workers, and Paper Workers; and building trades unions, such as the Laborers, Operating Engineers, Sheet Metal Workers, and, at that point in the campaign, the Carpenters.

My running mates represented the new American workforce. For secretary-treasurer, we nominated Rich Trumka, a third-generation coal miner from Nemacolin, Pennsylvania, who led the United Mine Workers. Rich began working in the mines at the age of nineteen, earning money for college and law school. Soon he became an activist in his union's reform movement, Miners for Democracy, which was led by the late, legendary Jock Yablonski. After four years on the union's legal staff, during the reform administration of Arnold Miller, Rich returned to the mines in 1978. And in 1982, at the age of thirty-three, he was elected the youngest president in the union's history.

Rich led two major strikes against the nation's coal companies — Pittston in 1989 and the Bituminous Coal Operators in 1993. A shrewd strategist, he mobilized support from the strikes among workers and their allies in this country — and even overseas. These battles brought about great gains in job security, pensions, and benefits. Once they saw the miners couldn't be beaten, the coal operators agreed to cooperate with the union to improve productivity.

Rich also led the fight to pass the Coal Act, which guarantees health care for 200,000 pensioners and widows, and got it enacted during the Bush administration. He tells two stories to explain why he's such a fanatic for health and safety.

First, his father suffers from black lung, a disease workers get from working in mines with unsafe levels of coal dust. One afternoon a few years ago, Rich's sister visited their father along with her three young sons. They asked if Grandpa could play ball with them, but he was too weak from black lung to toss a baseball around with his grandsons. Rich has a vivid memory from that afternoon of his father, sitting in his rocking chair, silhouetted against the window, unable to enjoy one of the simple pleasures of life.

And Rich himself was almost killed in a freak accident in a mine, when a coal car broke loose and rolled downhill. It killed a man who was working alongside Rich, and he died in Rich's arms. Such stories explain why Rich is sometimes the only dissenting vote on the president's Commission on Entitlements. Rich has seen firsthand how people risk their lives to earn a living.

Now forty-six, Rich bridges different generations — and different sections of the workforce. A student of labor history and a fan of 1960s rock music, he's worked as a laborer and as a lawyer. Rich can talk to anyone, from the coal fields to the college campuses, and given the slightest opportunity, he will talk to anyone. Recently, when he was in Birmingham, Alabama, for a hearing on why America needs a raise, he stopped on a rainy street, talked with several day laborers, and invited them to the hearing. One of those workers,

Wayne Bryant, later told a hushed hearing: "I'm homeless, but I'm not trying to hurt someone, rob them, or create problems. I was working for $4.25 an hour, but I couldn't pay my bills, buy groceries, gas, pay the electric bill, buy food, and take the kids to get clothes or to the hospital. I need to make more so I can live a productive and successful life. I'm not a criminal — give me a chance and I can do better."

For executive vice president — a new position — we nominated Linda Chavez-Thompson. The granddaughter of Mexican immigrants and one of eight children of sharecropper parents in Lubbock, Texas, she first started working summers in the cotton fields at the age of ten.

She became active in the labor movement in 1967, at the age of twenty-three, when she went to work for the Laborers local in Lubbock as the office secretary. She was instrumental in improving the efficiency of the local's hiring hall. In 1970, the Texas AFL-CIO asked her to do relief work after a tornado hit her hometown. Her organizing talent and her bilingual skills were invaluable for the effort.

Later that year she became a staff representative for the Laborers. Joining AFSCME as an organizer in 1971, she became director of the local in San Antonio, executive director of the Texas council, and a vice president of the national union. In these roles, she directed the union's efforts in a seven-state district — Arizona, Colorado, Nevada, New Mexico, Oklahoma, Texas, and Utah — that is usually regarded as unfriendly to labor. But, against the odds, she led an organizing drive that brought in five thousand new members in Texas in five years. And she helped pass a collective bargaining law for public employees in New Mexico.

As she moved into more activities on the national scene, she was elected as a national vice president of the Labor Council for Latin American Advancement in 1986, serving until 1996.

She also was elected to the AFL-CIO executive council, where I served with her and learned to respect her toughness, her practical intelligence, her wide-ranging experience, and her refusal to take anyone too seriously, including herself. That's why, when we were looking for someone to link the AFL-CIO with its grassroots activists and help "put the movement back in the labor movement," we knew that Linda was the person for the job. As she often says, she represents the workers the labor movement has often ignored: women, Latinos, workers in the Sunbelt, and recent immigrants and their children.

Kirkland soon announced his retirement, and Donahue announced his own candidacy, with the backing of Kirkland's supporters. Running against an old friend pained me, and Tom must have felt the same way, but our coalition did everything we could to make the election a decision about where labor was heading, not just about who would head labor. Our campaign developed a momentum that made it far more than a push for a slate of candidates. We called for far-reaching changes in the labor movement and generated growing excitement and grassroots support.

Calling for a "new voice" for American workers, we proposed an all-out effort to cure ourselves of the paralysis that gripped too much of our movement: the sense that we could not organize successfully in the absence of more favorable laws but could not change the law because we were too weak. Instead, we called for aggressive organizing on every front — in our industries, in the political arena, and in our attempts to win better contracts. Our goal was not just to win the election for the three candidates but to win with enough support to put our program through. We wanted a very public process to change the way people looked at unions, a process that involved activists across the country and attracted the attention of the news media. In this, we succeeded beyond our hopes, generating more news coverage than labor had received in memory.

At the AFL-CIO convention in New York City in October 1995, one measure of the excitement we generated was the turnout of delegates from labor's grassroots, the central labor councils representing unions in the states and in local communities. At the AFL-CIO convention in 1992, the central bodies had sent 186 delegates. In 1995, they sent 488 delegates — and three-quarters supported the New Voice slate.

These delegates helped elect a new — and more representative — leadership. After electing me as president and Rich Trumka as secretary-treasurer, the convention came together in support of a more inclusive leadership team. By unanimous votes, the delegates created the new office of executive vice president, as our coalition proposed, and elected Linda Chavez-Thompson. And, after negotiations between backers of our coalition and Tom Donahue's campaign, AFSCME President Gerald McEntee and UFCW President Douglas Dority presented a "unity slate" that expanded the executive council from 35 to 54, with the percentage of women and minorities rising from 17 to 27 percent.

Throughout the convention, the debate wasn't about whether to change — but how. Tom Donahue and his supporters joined us in calling for an expanded commitment to organizing, a tougher stance in the political arena, and more diversity in our leadership. In fact, Tom also helped break the "glass ceiling" at the AFL-CIO by nominating Barbara Easterling of the CWA as his running mate for secretary-treasurer.

We left the convention with a leadership that better reflects the face of America at work. One fact says it all: the late United Farm Workers' Cesar Chavez had never been chosen for labor's top decision-making group. But now his successor, Arturo Rodriguez, would serve on the council.[21]

And the AFL-CIO did more than change its leadership — we started talking to working Americans again. In my acceptance speech, I began our dialogue with working Americans with four simple words: "America needs a raise."

We were changing the labor movement, but, more important, we were beginning the work of changing America. That work continues with an unprecedented effort to bring working people's concerns to the forefront of public debate in the 1996 elections — and an all-out campaign to organize the new American workforce for years to come.

CHAPTER 4

People Politics

THE CENTRAL ECONOMIC REALITY of our time is that working people's wages have been in free fall for twenty years or more. The central social reality is that falling family incomes and growing inequality are tearing at the fabric of our society, from the safety of our neighborhoods to the quality of our schools. And the central political reality is that people are losing faith in the ability of the democratic process and government at every level to help lift their living standards and restore their way of life.

In national elections, the "swing voters" are working people whose wages are declining and who are searching for a political home. During the 1980s, many of these voters became Reagan Democrats. In 1992, some supported Ross Perot's independent candidacy, while more swung the election to Bill Clinton. In 1994, many switched to Republican congressional candidates, and others simply stayed home.

In 1996 and beyond, economically anxious voters hold the future of American politics in their hands — the same hands that work on assembly lines and construction sites, at computer terminals and supermarket check-out lines. These voters look at the political system and conclude, "Nobody speaks for me." Too often, they're right.

For instance, during 1995 and early 1996, politicians from both parties were debating the federal budget, the shutdown of the federal government, and such emotionally charged social issues as affirmative action, immigration, and violence on TV and in the movies. But many politicians ignored the most urgent problem: people found their jobs endangered by corporate downsizings, and they hadn't had a raise in years.

To be sure, Labor Secretary Robert Reich, Senator Edward Kennedy, House Democratic leaders Richard Gephardt and David Bonior, and the labor movement all tried to raise the issues of jobs and wages. But the political establishment and most of the major media didn't pay attention until the conservative commentator Patrick Buchanan started pounding podiums about it in his insurgent campaign for the Republican presidential nomination.[1] And the day before Buchanan's victory in the New Hampshire primary, his leading rival, Senate Republican leader Bob Dole, said, "I didn't realize jobs and trade and what makes America work would become a big issue in the last days of this campaign."

Dole's statement exemplifies what infuriates Americans about too many politicians: their isolation from the realities of earning a living in America today. The sense that the political system is isolated, ignorant, and indifferent to the struggles of working Americans creates a dangerous vacuum. And sometimes that vacuum is filled by extremists.

In Louisiana in 1990, a disturbingly large number of working-class voters supported the "former" Ku Klux Klansman David Duke for United States senator. Many voters were drawn to Duke more by his phony populism than his heartfelt hate-mongering. A survey of Democrats who supported Duke found that 63 percent said the middle class is more severely squeezed by "tax breaks for the rich and unfair advantages for big business" than by "the cost of welfare programs for the poor and unfair advantages for minorities." For some voters, Duke was filling a vacuum created by the absence of aggressive advocates for working families.[2]

My vision of the labor movement is that we can be the voice that fills this vacuum. Just as we need to find new ways to represent our current members and organize new members, we need to find more effective ways to fight in the political arena for all working people. Revitalizing the labor movement is like weaving a seamless garment of activism — organizing campaigns, contract campaigns, and political campaigns.

A revitalized labor movement can bridge the gap between working people whose living standards are stagnating and those who also work hard but have been shut out of middle-class security. We can bring working people together, mobilize the potential power of their great numbers, and hold political leaders accountable to their concerns. We can prove that organized people can prevail over organized money. And when we do that, we will help working people lift their living standards — and help all Americans restore the vitality and legitimacy of our democratic process.

Swing Voters: Anxious, Angry, and Alienated

In recent elections, the voters whose decisions made the difference have been working people anxious about their jobs and living standards.

Political analyst Ruy Teixeira of the Economic Policy Institute has studied the voters who swung from George Bush in 1988 to Bill Clinton and Ross Perot in 1992 — and from

Democratic congressional candidates in 1992 to Republicans
in 1994.[3] Overwhelmingly, these voters were working people
in the middle of the economic and educational spectrum —
people who had graduated from high school but did not have
a four-year college degree. They responded to a prolonged
period of economic insecurity: the four years of the Bush
presidency, when a recession swelled unemployment and
drove down wages, and the first two years of the Clinton
administration, when an economic recovery created millions
of new jobs while wages continued to stagnate. Thus, from
1992 to 1994, Democratic support fell eleven points among
high school graduates and twelve points among those with
some college, as real wages for both groups continued to
drop. But Democratic backing held steady among college
graduates, whose earnings rose during the recovery.

Most postelection analyses attributed the Republican congressional victory in 1994 to "angry white men" who were
supposedly enraged about social issues — crime, immigration, affirmative action, and gun control. As someone who's
argued about these issues in union halls and on picket lines,
I'd be the last to deny that they get all kinds of people hot
under the collar. But I'd suggest that the central issue in
American politics is whether American workers can afford to
maintain the American way of life. That is the issue which
moves working women and men from every racial and ethnic
group. And that is why the swing away from whichever party
is in power — away from the Republicans in 1992 and away
from the Democrats in 1994 — was greatest among those
whose paychecks were pinched.

For all the talk about angry white men, an equally important group could be called the "anxious working women."
Among white women with high school diplomas and those

with some college but not a degree, support for Democrats dropped 10 percent in 1994. (Although African-American turnout declined, the percentage of Democratic support held steady among those who voted.) In a memo, written in the spring of 1995, explaining the fall-off of Democratic support among women, the public opinion analyst Celinda Lake noted: "While 42% of men believe the economy is in recovery, only 30% of women agree. . . . Negative impressions of the economy may also have depressed turnout among women — 72% of nonvoters felt the economy was not in good shape."

Moreover, some economically anxious voters expressed their disillusionment with the Democrats not by voting Republican but simply by staying home. In a postelection survey, the Clinton White House pollster Stanley Greenberg found: "Last year's nonvoters — people who stayed home but who had voted for president in 1992 — were largely noncollege graduates under 50 years of age. They were disproportionately downscale Democrats who strongly favored Democratic congressional candidates to Republicans. Unfortunately, they were not sufficiently energized to vote." You might say they had conducted an electoral sit-down strike.

Nonvoting is part of a larger pattern of citizen cynicism. By 1994, only 18 percent of all Americans trusted Congress, compared with 24 percent in 1990 and 39 percent in 1985. Yet only one-quarter trusted government in general, compared to three-quarters in 1964. Voters watched their living standards decline while politicians in Washington bickered among themselves or offered special favors to the wealthy and well connected. They understood that, in today's political process, money doesn't just talk — it shouts. And the voice of corporate America drowns out the voice of the people. That is why, in a recent survey, 80 percent said the government is run for "special interests, not the people."

When you listen to working Americans who are losing faith in the political process, you keep hearing about the same problems. Working families are having a hard time paying their bills and finding time to spend with their children. They're concerned about getting home safely from work every evening. They worry that their kids are exposed to drugs and guns, even in school. It's hard to categorize these concerns as "values" or "economics," "liberal" or "conservative." They're a web of social and economic anxieties whose common thread is uneasiness about the loss of a way of life in which working families once enjoyed dignity, opportunity, and security.

Listen to a pipefitter and union member from Cleveland, who describes himself as "a conservative Democrat." His views are shaped by the problems that are part of his life — crime, taxes, and the rising cost of living. He understands — and understandably resents — the fact that most politicians are insulated from the difficulties and dangers of working people's lives:

> If you take the average union members, I think most would probably call themselves conservative Democrats because we have to be conservative. We don't go out and freely spend our money every week. We are trying to pinch pennies to meet our budgets and everything else, and then we end up electing people who get in office and don't really represent our values.
>
> They believe that you don't need a gun. The average working man probably feels he needs to have a gun. He might [live or work] in a neighborhood where he might get attacked. He feels he has a right to defend his property. But we elect Democrats who live out somewhere real nice where they don't need a gun,

and they want to tell you you shouldn't have one. . . . That is why a lot of unions started voting Republican, which I feel is not the smart thing to do.[4]

Another aspect of the alienation of working-class voters was expressed by a teacher in Cleveland's public schools, who says that people she knows

> probably don't see any differences between a Democratic Congress and a Republican Congress. I mean, there are differences, but when it comes to corporations, the Democratic Congress also did the same. What I am saying is, basically, corporations used to give money to Democratic candidates and they also give money to Republican candidates, so that whoever gets elected, they will benefit each way.[5]

Labor's Muffled Voice

The challenge for a revitalized labor movement is to offer a voice for the pipefitter and the teacher. But too often our voice has been muffled. With more than thirteen million members all across America, the labor movement is still a formidable political force. Political candidates seek our support; our members vote more heavily, and more in keeping with their economic interests, than other working Americans; and our enemies devote lots of time and energy to attacking — and also imitating — us.

Our shrewdest adversaries understand our historic accomplishments, our potential power, and our recent failures. The executive director of the influential and ultraconservative Christian Coalition, Ralph Reed, has said that his movement is "doing the same kind of grassroots . . . organizing that labor unions did in the '30s and '40s."

The 1994 elections were a wake-up call for the labor movement. The percentage of union members voting Democratic dropped from 70 percent in 1990 to 61 percent in 1994. The president of the Machinists' union, George Kourpias, said simply, "Anyone who tells you we didn't lose our members in '94 is crazy." The fall-off in Democratic support, of course, was even greater among nonunion voters.

The point isn't that fewer union members voted Democratic — the mission of our movement is to empower working families, not to elect politicians from a particular party. The point is that working people stood by or even helped elect politicians indifferent or hostile to their interests and values.

What's gone wrong with organized labor is similar to what's gone wrong with so many other organizations whose hearts are in the right place but whose minds have become complacent and whose muscles have gotten flabby. Too often, our idea of legislative and political action has degenerated into writing checks to political candidates and party organizations, lobbying entrenched members of Congress, and — shortly before Election Day — sending mailings to union members informing them of our endorsements.

The result is that the labor movement has failed to fill a vacuum in American politics. Working people feel that no one's speaking out on the issues that shape their lives and their children's futures. Union members, in particular, want the labor movement to keep them informed about what public officials are doing, or are failing to do, on such matters as jobs, wages, Social Security, health care, and education and training.

Speaking out for working Americans and keeping our members informed — this is what the labor movement should be doing, not just writing checks. Anyway, "checkbook politics" has become less and less effective at winning legislative battles in Washington — or political battles all across America. After all, the labor movement's strength should be our members, not our money. There will always be a great gap between the donations of working men and women and the contributions from corporate coffers. In 1992 and again in 1994, labor's political action committees spent about $42 million, compared with more than $130 million spent by business during each campaign.[6] Where we fell short was not in failing to contribute money but in failing to communicate our message to our members and to all working people. Even before we lost the 1994 congressional elections, we were losing important battles in Congress.

In 1992 we helped elect Bill Clinton, and helped return Democratic majorities in both houses of Congress. To be sure, with the help of the president and the congressional leaders, we won some long-overdue victories in Congress: family and medical leave, tax credits for working families, and improvements in education, from Head Start to job training and college loans. Yet on some of the issues that matter most to working people, it was hard to tell our "friends" from our "enemies."

For more than a decade, corporate America upset the balance between employers and employees by firing working people who went on strike to preserve their pay and benefits. But we were unable to find enough Democratic support in the United States Senate to enact a law prohibiting the permanent replacement of striking workers. Similarly, President Clinton could not persuade the Democratic majority in Congress to pass his plan for health-care coverage for every American family. I headed the AFL-CIO's effort for health-care reform, and I give Clinton a great deal of credit for fighting so long and hard for an issue of such importance to working Americans.

Largely because it was investing so much political capital in health-care reform, the Clinton administration didn't propose an increase in the minimum wage during 1993 and 1994, when Democrats controlled both houses of Congress. After two years during which working people had relatively little to show from their friends, it is not surprising that, with their abstentions and even their votes, they helped elect their enemies. Now that we in the labor movement are reexamining, reforming, and revitalizing ourselves, the question is: how can we do better?

No More Politics As Usual

Angry, anxious, and alienated voters — many of whom are union members — have a clear message for the labor movement. When we participate in politics, we shouldn't act as one more special interest group. We need to act as a social movement that represents working people throughout the society — union members and nonmembers alike. That way, we can fill the gaping vacuum in American political life: the need for a movement that listens to, speaks for, and fights for people who work for a living.

Union members understand the difference between what we are — and what we must become. In a survey of union members, fully two-thirds said it is important for their unions to be involved in national politics, trying to elect candidates who are pro-worker. Their quarrel isn't with our mission but with our methods.

That is why only 38 percent say they're satisfied with what the labor movement is doing now. In presenting these findings, the public opinion analysts Geoffrey Garin and Guy Molyneux reported, "Members too often perceive unions as pursuing a largely ineffective strategy — namely, trying to gain influence inside a failed political system by cultivating relationships with the Democratic Party or with specific candidates." They concluded that union members want political action to be something different and better: "a way of giving working people a place and a voice in a political debate that now excludes them."

That means building an independent movement that mobilizes working people, raises their issues in public debate, and brings their concerns before public officials — every year, not just election years, and all year round, not just during campaign seasons. During campaigns, we should offer union members the information they need to make intelligent decisions; we should not tell them to vote for candidates because they're Democrats or because they carry the unions' endorsements. We need to become a kind of *Consumer Reports* for working families on legislative issues, public officials, and political candidates.

In short, we need to be political watchdogs, not political lapdogs. And restoring our independence will make us more effective than tethering ourselves to a political party. As we help workers organize themselves in their workplaces, as we fight to win union members better pay and benefits, and as we fight for such issues as raising the minimum wage and protecting workers' health and safety, we will earn a new credibility with our members and with all working people. That credibility will make the information we offer more believable — and our endorsements more valuable.

Think about it: if you were buying a car, whose advice would you follow? A fast-talking salesman like Joe Isuzu? Or a respected source of information like *Consumer Reports*?

Political Organizing

I've told you about the first time I gave a political speech — and felt as awkward as a youngster on his first date.

It was a Saturday afternoon in the Bronx, just before Election Day, and a few of my father's union buddies were letting me ride around in their sound truck. When we stopped at a shopping center, one crusty old bus driver handed me the microphone and said, "Kid, why don't you talk to the people?" As I started speaking, my amplified voice echoed back to me — and I've hardly ever heard anyone sound so scared.

During my first days as president of the AFL-CIO, I thought back to that moment. Our new leadership team had just been handed one of the most powerful microphones in American politics. And our challenge was to make sure that working people's voices would be heard loud and clear. Fortunately, we were better prepared than I'd been as a kid in the Bronx. Among the issues we'd thrashed out in our New Voice campaign was how we could build workers' power in the political process.

Our leading strategist for the political program was Gerry McEntee, the president of the state and local government employees' union, AFSCME. He had grown up in Philadelphia, the son of an organizer who kept rising in the union's leadership, from the local to the state and national levels. At his family's dinner table, Gerry learned this lesson: working folks have to fight as hard in the political process as on the picket lines and bargaining tables. With Gerry's aggressive leadership we put together a plan for the labor movement to speak up for working families and help our members learn about the issues at stake in 1996. Our plan was approved at a special convention of the AFL-CIO in March 1996.

In essence, we're going to bring the same organizing vision to the political world that we bring to the workplace.

We want to begin a national discussion about the problems of jobs, wages, and an economy that no longer seems to respect workers or reward their dedication, effort, and skill. We are mobilizing working Americans around the problems that touch their lives, bringing their concerns to the attention of their elected representatives, and raising an issue-oriented standard by which they can measure candidates. To accomplish these goals, we are building a nationwide grassroots network to carry working people's voices into political debate. Our slogan is simply "America needs a raise."

For starters, we held a series of town hall meetings in thirty cities, where working men and women addressed the most urgent issue in 1996 and beyond: the growing gap in wages and wealth between working families and the wealthy. We are also raising these issues over the nation's airwaves, with national television and radio advertisements. These messages spotlight the squeeze on working families, and they answer the attack on working families by the Republican majorities in Congress who are trying to cut Medicare, Medicaid, education, job safety, and health and pension protections, while giving new tax breaks to big business and the rich.

Already, our efforts have pushed the issue of raising the minimum wage to the forefront of public debate. During

April 1996, the AFL-CIO broadcast television and radio ads in some thirty congressional districts where representatives from both parties hesitated to support an increase in the minimum wage. In these messages and with our efforts at grassroots organizing, we made the point that the minimum wage amounts to $8800 a year — well below the poverty level of $15,000 for a family of four. And, at a time when corporate profits and executive salaries are soaring, people who work full time should not be forced to live in poverty.

With public opinion surveys showing that more than three-quarters of all Americans supported an increase in the minimum wage, a growing number of Republican members of Congress broke ranks with their party's leadership to support the idea. (As I finish this book, the outcome of the issue was unclear, but it *was* clear that the American people were compelling their representatives to address the issue of making work pay.)

If these messages are our "air war," our most important fight will be our "ground war" — our effort to build a grassroots movement of working families all across America. We're sending an army of organizers to all congressional districts with large numbers of union members — and with representatives whose records show the failure to represent the needs of working families.

The organizers are talking to working people about the issues that matter most — the economy, jobs, wages, health care, pensions, and college loans. They're asking hundreds of union members to pledge to spend thirty hours this year taking the message to friends, neighbors, and co-workers that America needs a raise and public policies that offer more opportunity and security for working families. And — through letter-writing campaigns, meetings with members of

Congress, and "accountability sessions" where constituents confront their representatives — they'll ask Congress to do right by the people who have sent them to Washington.

People Politics Works

During the fall of 1996, the organizers and the volunteers they've recruited will let people know about their representatives' records. The 1996 elections will be a referendum on whether Americans want public officials and public policies that lift working families up — or drive them down.

In reporting our planned efforts, the news media have headlined our estimated cost for the campaign: a one-time $35 million commitment from the current budgets of the national unions, with the largest unions making special contributions.

In fact, for a year we're devoting fifteen cents per month out of the dues the members already pay to their unions so that we can talk about issues important to working families. That's a relatively low cost for a great goal: making sure that working people have a voice in this year's debates. By way of comparison, just one multimillionaire, Steve Forbes, spent about $30 million of his inherited fortune to make his voice heard during the Republican presidential primaries this year.

Yes, we are making an extra effort this year. But it isn't an exercise in "checkbook politics." None of the money is being contributed to political candidates or political parties. Instead, we're devoting our effort to information, education, and mobilization, so that we can build political power for working Americans. That's our goal — not to elect Democrats or Republicans.

We've already had a trial run for a political strategy that

treats election campaigns as opportunities to educate and mobilize working families. In January 1996, labor helped to elect the first Democratic senator from Oregon in many years. Veteran Republican Senator Bob Packwood had retired in disgrace, and his successor was being chosen by the first-ever mail ballot for a seat in either house of Congress. The race was between Democratic Representative Ron Wyden, who had a strong record on workers' issues, and State Senate President Gordon Smith, a multimillionaire businessman. Smith outspent Wyden by $1.1 million — and supplied $2 million out of his own pocket — but labor's campaign matched people power against money power. In a tryout of labor's plans for grassroots organizing, more than five hundred union members volunteered to help. They made phone calls and sent informational literature to every union member in Oregon.

The mailings featured specific information about the candidates' positions on the minimum wage, worker safety, Medicare, education, and environmental protection. After the voting period began, union activists tracked which members had voted by regularly checking records at local election offices. Then they concentrated their phone calls and mailings on those who had not yet mailed in their ballots. In addition, hundreds of union activists also volunteered in the Wyden campaign, joining in "labor walks" on weekends, strolling through their communities and leafleting and speaking with people. As AFSCME activist Mary Botkin recalled: "This was not an Election Day — this was an election month. Our volunteers had to turn out again and again, and they did, sometimes going door to door when the wind chill was 10 degrees below zero, and in high winds and torrential rains."

On a visit to Oregon, AFL-CIO Secretary-Treasurer Rich

Trumka joined a Wyden labor walk by 120 volunteers in five inches of snow. The AFL-CIO executive vice president, Linda Chavez-Thompson, led a labor rally for Wyden. The rumpled, energetic Wyden wore the union label on his sleeve, joining Trumka on a Machinists' picket line and touring various unionized work sites, including a shipyard, a steel mill, and a hospital.

When the votes were counted, Wyden had won by some seventeen thousand votes — and union members had made the difference. Postelection surveys showed that, in some counties, union members' turnout was as much as 11 percent higher than the overall record level of 65 percent. Teamsters members voted by an estimated 62 percent to 38 percent for Wyden, although only 51 percent were registered Democrats.

Oregon's message was simple but powerful: grassroots organizing is good politics. And workers' issues are winning issues.

Money Power vs. People Power

As the 1996 campaign unfolds, it will test the strength of organized working people against organized corporate money. The new Republican Congress, including the freshman representatives who came to Washington promising to reform politics, are setting new records for raking in corporate money.

According to a study by the consumer group Citizen Action, Republicans in the House of Representatives collected $57.9 million in campaign contributions in 1995, overwhelmingly from corporate political action committees and wealthy donors — for an average of $246,331 per member. In comparison, Democrats received $36.7 million in contributions

— for an average of $184,633 per member.[7] The Republicans' fund-raising bonanza was no accident. Right after winning the 1994 elections, Speaker-elect Newt Gingrich and Bill Paxon, chairman of the National Republican Congressional Committee, warned corporate lobbyists against continuing to contribute to Democrats. What was more alarming, the House Republicans asked corporate campaign contributors to help them rewrite regulations protecting working people, consumers, and the natural environment.

Led by the majority whip, Tom DeLay, House Republicans set up Project Relief to promote "regulatory reform." More than thirty-five business groups contributed $5.36 million, according to the Center for Responsive Politics.[8]

These regulatory issues may sound complex, but they can be matters of life and death for working families. For instance, the nation's leading PAC contributor is the United Parcel Service, Inc., with a war chest of more than $2 million a year. UPS is also number one in worker complaints about job safety problems, according to the federal Occupational Safety and Health Administration. In fact, in a typical recent year, 1992, UPS workers suffered 10,555 lifting and lowering injuries that required more than first aid. The problem is so bad that, on February 7, 1994, Teamsters president Ron Carey, a former UPS driver himself, led a one-day national UPS strike because the company was increasing its maximum package weight from 70 to 150 pounds, without bargaining with the union over safety precautions. As a result of the strike, the same afternoon UPS agreed that no worker would be required to handle a package over 70 pounds without help from another worker, as well as appropriate lifting devices. Not surprisingly, UPS uses its political and legislative clout to push for easing the OSHA standards, especially those for cumulative stress disorders caused by repetitive motion or lifting. More than 180,000 UPS workers are at risk of these injuries, driving trucks or handling packages.[9]

Similarly, Republican-backed legislation cutting corporate penalties for emitting toxic waste was written by lobbyists from the American Petroleum Institute. Corporate political action committees from the oil and gas industry gave $3.9 million to Republicans in 1994 and $1.23 million in the first six months of 1995.

The American Bankers Association gave $680,000 to Republican congressional candidates in 1994. Maybe it's no accident that the new Republican majority voted to eliminate the direct student loan program, which allows students to borrow from the government rather than seek government-guaranteed loans from the banks.[10]

Shredding the Safety Net?

The corporation-funded attack on working families raises a larger issue for 1996 and beyond, an issue that explains why working people must rebuild their political power. At a time when business is downsizing workers' jobs and raises, more families depend on America's safety net, the web of programs and legal protections that offers people a measure of security when they fall on hard times. So, is this the time to shred the safety net — now that more Americans are in danger of dropping through it?

For instance, forty million Americans, most of them working people and their families, now have no health insurance at all — a big jump from thirty-one million in 1987. Similarly, the growing number of victims of corporate downsizing —

such as the forty thousand workers losing their jobs at AT&T — may eventually depend on unemployment insurance. Yet the unemployment insurance system now covers only 35 percent of jobless workers, compared with 65 percent in 1975.

Fewer workers have good employer-provided retirement plans. The number of workers covered by low-risk defined-benefit plans dropped 30 percent from 1981 through 1991. That is why unemployment insurance, Medicaid and Medicare, and federal pension protections are more important than ever before. So are the other programs that make up the safety net: Social Security, minimum-wage laws, Aid to Families with Dependent Children, consumer protection, clean air and water, job safety and health, and workers' rights to overtime pay, to name just a few.

Yet these and other programs are in danger from the new congressional majority, which seems intent on tilting the balance of power between corporate America and working America even more in favor of big business. Here's one example of what's at stake.

Wage-and-hour laws that have been in place since the 1930s would be weakened with the repeal of the forty-hour week. That means you couldn't be sure of getting paid for time-and-a-half if you worked more than those forty hours a week. That's a real danger at a time when people are working longer hours just to pay their bills — and companies are working employees harder rather than hiring additional ones.

Similarly, the new congressional majority is considering repealing two long-established laws that make sure the taxpayers' dollars will be used to build a strong economy by paying decent wages to employees of federal contractors. The Davis-Bacon Act covers construction workers on federally funded projects, and the Service Contract Act covers security guards, janitors, and food service workers, among other employees of federal contractors. Here, too, the new congressional majority seems intent on driving wages down.

As we spread the message about what's at stake this year and in the years ahead, we'll be telling working Americans the frightening truth: not only are your jobs in danger and your paychecks shrinking, but if you fall on hard times, there may not be a safety net to catch you.

Rooting Politics in Reality

As we build a new movement of working families, we're going to do more than play defense. We're going to change the nature of politics itself, so that working people can set the agenda, run for and win public office, and teach public officials some lessons about the daily realities of most families' lives.

This year, we're training some three thousand union activists in how to participate more effectively in political and legislative campaigns. You've seen and heard political hired-guns on TV, bragging about how they produce "messages" and "get-out-the-vote" and other tricks of the trade. That's what we're teaching, and you're going to see some steelworkers, teachers, auto workers, health-care workers, and telephone operators beating those political operators at their own game.

We're also finding out how many union members already hold public office or are planning to run for office, and we'll try to help them out. We'll be recruiting more members to run for public office, starting with local positions like the school board and the county commission. It's time for licensed prac-

tical nurses and machinists — not just lawyers and million-
aires — to run for and win public office.

As long as there are professional politicians, we're going to
do our best to help them learn a little about how most Americans live and work and scramble to stay even. We're going to
start a school for political candidates, so that they can hear
about working people's problems from the best teachers of all
— working people who are struggling to make a living. We'll
even give diplomas to the candidates — after they've completed a day's work of listening to and learning from working
folks.

We're working to raise wages at the local level, too. In
efforts that are models for the kind of social movement we
want to build, labor unions and their allies are urging city
governments to raise the minimum wage in their communities, either for employees of municipal contractors or for
all working people. Baltimore, Milwaukee, and Santa Clara
County, California, have already passed "living wage" meas-
ures, and similar efforts are under way in communities including Denver, New York City, New Orleans, Chicago, and
Los Angeles.

As we participate more energetically and effectively, we'll
perform a real service to the political process: we'll root it in
reality. By emphasizing the vital issues facing every working
family — jobs, wages, pensions, health care, and education
and training — we'll take some of the edge off the issues, like
immigration and affirmative action, that too many politicians
use to divide Americans against each other. We'll also give
political leaders — and the insulated professionals who staff
their campaigns and administrations — more details about
the problems people experience and the help they need. Lord
knows, the political establishment in both parties can use a
remedial course in paycheck economics.

Earlier, I told you how Bob Dole was amazed that jobs could be an issue in the presidential campaign. In fairness, ignorance and isolation are problems in both parties. For instance, there's a group of self-styled "centrists" within the Democratic Party that calls itself the Democratic Leadership Council. They aren't all out of touch or off the wall — Dick Gephardt was one of their founders, and Bill Clinton once was their chair. But their full-time leaders and staff seem fixated on the ideas that working people are a "special interest" the Democratic Party should shuck off and that corporate America is a constituency the Democrats should woo.

The DLC publishes a magazine called *The New Democrat,* and its July–August 1995 issue was a perfect example of the kind of ignorance we have to weed out of the Democratic Party as well as the Republican Party. In an editorial entitled "The Death of Machine Age Politics," the DLC attacked the Clinton administration for positioning

> the Democratic Party as the champion of embattled interest groups opposing social and economic change. It's hard to find any other characterization of Vice President Al Gore's mission earlier this year to . . . appease organized labor with offers of a minimum-wage hike, a ban on replacing strikers, and opposition to sensible labor law reforms that would allow a more participatory workplace.[11]

By "sensible labor law reforms," they didn't mean prohibiting employers from firing employees for organizing; they meant getting rid of the sixty-year ban on employer-dominated "company unions."

In another article, entitled, "Beyond Repair: The Politics of the Machine Age Are Hopelessly Obsolete," Michael Rothschild offered some opinions that make Pollyanna sound like a pessimist:

Thanks to the near-miraculous capabilities of microelectronics, we are vanquishing scarcity. . . . The losers this time are those who cannot or will not participate in the Knowledge Age economy. . . . Like illiterate peasants in the Age of Steam, today's unskilled are being left behind by the new economy. . . . Other than the poorest 20 percent of Americans whose illiteracy prevents their participation in the Knowledge Age, everyone senses the promise of the new economy.[12]

In fact, 80 percent of Americans are not gliding blissfully into some post-scarcity utopia. Eighty percent of Americans are losing ground economically. And, as for the *New Democrat*'s dismissal of most working people as "illiterate peasants," that phrase came back to bite the political establishment when Pat Buchanan offered himself as the candidate of "peasants with pitchforks" against economic, cultural, and political elites.

A new movement of working people can offer Americans something better than politics that ignore or exploit most people's pain. We can restore the most basic elements of democracy — ordinary citizens' ability to speak out and be heard, to organize themselves and influence public decisions, to elect public officials and hold them accountable, to seek and win public office and build a power base of their own. For too long, what's been missing from American politics is the voice of working Americans. By restoring that voice, we will do something more important than revive the Democratic Party; we will renew the democratic process.

CHAPTER 5

Changing Lives, Changing America

OVER THE PAST forty years, the top leaders of the AFL-CIO met every February in Bal Harbour, a beachfront resort just north of Miami. Usually, the meetings covered routine union business, interspersed with visits from prominent political leaders. The news media presented the sessions as symbols of the labor federation's complacency — often with photos of older men lounging at poolside.

But our February 1996 meeting was different. It was the first meeting of the AFL-CIO Executive Council since our new leadership team took office — and our last meeting in Bal Harbour. From now on, we'll meet in communities where major organizing drives or contract battles are taking place.

The business before us was anything but routine. We were beginning the job of rebuilding a movement of, by, and for working Americans. And the first speakers were union activists, fresh from the frontlines of organizing campaigns.[1] One speaker, Bob Gorman, is organizing electricians and other skilled building trades workers. He's business manager of Local 146 of the International Brotherhood of Electrical

Workers (IBEW) in Seattle. As a result of the organizing drive, the union has increased its "market share" to almost three-quarters of the construction projects in the Seattle area. That means the new members are earning higher wages, while long-time members have less reason to fear that contractors will replace them with low-wage workers.

Another organizer, Gail Floyd, is on a similar mission. She works on high-tech communications for AT&T in Jackson-ville, Florida, and she's a volunteer for her CWA local union, organizing throughout the industry, from nonunion divisions of AT&T to service representatives for US Air. "With two small kids and a full-time job, volunteer organizing isn't easy," she said. But she's making her own job at AT&T a little more secure by making it more difficult for companies to compete by driving down their employees' pay.

Yet another organizer, Shirley Aldebol, joined AFSCME as a social worker in the welfare department in New York City. Now, she's organizing public employees in Puerto Rico. She's struggling with a bitter irony: too often, people who work in welfare offices in Puerto Rico earn so little that they qualify for public assistance themselves. So she spends much of her time providing essential services for single mothers who are working at poverty wages — helping them find child care or apply for food stamps to supplement their pay-checks.

Another speaker, Yamira Merino, came to this country from El Salvador just one year ago. She's one of 150 workers, mostly immigrants, who organized their Los Angeles shrimp-processing plant, with help from the Laborers union. As Me-rino spoke, her co-workers were embroiled in another battle: to bargain their first union contract and improve their pay and working conditions.

A "Seamless Garment" of Activism

Shirley Aldebol, Bob Gorman, Gail Floyd, and Yamira Merino represent some of the scope and the sweep of our effort to offer working people a strong new voice. Here's why that effort is so important.

For every problem plaguing working Americans, the common element is that they have too little power over their lives and livelihoods. For instance, as long as most working people lack leverage over their employers, they'll have a hard time winning wage increases. And, as long as labor laws are tilted toward employers, building unions in most workplaces will be difficult — not impossible, but difficult. Until working people have a stronger voice in national politics, we will never be able to change the laws.

That is why the solution to working people's problems, small and large, is, to borrow a phrase from people of faith, a "seamless garment" of activism. It means organizing for economic security and social justice in our workplaces, in our communities, and at every level of the political process. And that means building a new movement of working people.

The movement of working people that I envision can improve our lives and change America for the better by:

- Organizing entire industries, increasing wages, improving benefits and conditions — and sending ripples of pay raises throughout the economy.
- Building social movements that reach beyond the workplace into the entire community and offer working people beyond our ranks the opportunity to improve their lives and livelihoods.

- Meeting the full range of needs of workers in the new economy; addressing the special concerns of people in different industries and occupations and becoming a source of education and training.
- Offering working people new ways to protect their job security and lift their living standards, even in the face of attacks from powerful corporations.
- Forging a new social contract under which working people will enjoy a greater share of the wealth they produce, as well as a stronger voice in improving the quality of the products they make and the services they provide.
- And renewing the spirit of community in America by bridging the divisions of color and culture and restoring the sense that work is respected and rewarded.

Organizing Industries and Communities

When I talk with union people around the country, the first question I ask is, "How's the organizing going?" The most important thing we can do is to assist working men and women who are organizing for raises, rights, and respect. That's the best way to improve the pay and prospects of all Americans who are struggling to make ends meet, whether or not they're currently members of unions.

Union representation is still the surest guarantee that working people can earn a decent living. In private industry, union members earn $14.42 an hour, compared with $11.90 an hour for nonunion workers. Union members enjoy an even greater edge in benefits — $7.99 an hour, compared to only $4.35 an hour for workers without union representation. And — for union members and nonmembers alike — the greater the proportion of workers who are organized in a particular industry in a particular community, the higher wages are for everyone. For instance, a recent study at the University of Wisconsin found that, for every 10 percent increase in unionization in the retail food industry, there is a 2.3 percent increase in wages. Wages in the construction industry also rise as the percentage of workers with union representation increases. The AFL-CIO's Building and Construction Trades Department, under the leadership of Bob Georgine, and Laborers union president Arthur Coia, who chairs the AFL-CIO's Committee on Organizing, are emphasizing this fact in their efforts to build support among union members for expanded organizing efforts.

In the past, union members won improvements in pay and benefits that set the pace for working people throughout the economy. However — now that the labor movement represents only about 16 percent of the entire workforce and 11 percent of working people in private industry — there's the danger that, instead of unions lifting all working people up, nonunion employers will drag all working people down.

Whether you're an electrician, a nurse, a janitor, or a data-processing specialist — to name just a few occupations — you can't count on continuing to earn a decent living if someone down the street is doing the same job as you do at a poverty wage. That's why, if you work for a living, you have a stake in rebuilding a strong movement of working people, whether or not you currently belong to a union.

Labor's new leaders are doing everything they can to help working people organize themselves in their offices, factories, stores, schools, and construction sites. At the AFL-CIO, for the first time in its history, we've created a new Organizing Department, with a $20 million fund, to help unions reach out to working people in their industries. We're expanding our Organizing Institute so that it can recruit and train a thousand rank-and-file union members, recent college graduates, and other concerned and capable people to serve as union organizers. And we're challenging unions at every level to invest 30 percent or more of their budgets in organizing.

When I talk to union audiences, I often say that I want to revive "the culture of organizing" within the labor movement. That's just one way of saying that unions should look outward, not inward. We need to carry on a continuing conversation with working people and employers who aren't covered by union contracts. We need to help people who are interested in organizing where they work. And we should spare no effort to improve pay, benefits, and conditions for working people throughout the economy.

That kind of labor movement will be more helpful for every working woman and man, already a union member or not. Current members will benefit because unions that organize are more familiar with conditions throughout their industries, command more respect from employers, and exert more influence in their communities. Most important of all, these unions defend their members' job security and pay scales by protecting them against companies that compete by driving down wages and benefits. As for working people who still aren't union members, a labor movement focused on organizing can help you make your job better.

With an army of organizers — from youthful activists to experienced shop stewards — we can do what the labor movement did decades ago: organize workers and raise wages in entire industries. For instance, in 1937, the Steel Workers Organizing Committee — the forerunner of the United Steelworkers — had more than five thousand organizers, from full-time staff to volunteers. At its peak in 1937, the Textile

Workers Organizing Committee, a forerunner of UNITE, deployed 650 organizers throughout the country. Thanks to their efforts — and the struggle and sacrifice of tens of thousands of working people — steelworkers, textile workers, and workers in other industries were able to lift themselves and their families into the middle class for several of the most prosperous decades in American history. They shared their good fortune with entire communities, from the supermarkets and department stores where they shopped to the school systems they supported with their tax dollars. And, filled with love and loyalty for the country that offered them a dignified life, working Americans defeated fascism in World War II and contained communism in the Cold War.

Now, we're trying to help a new generation of working Americans accomplish the same things for their families, their communities, and their country. This is a promising moment for working people to organize themselves and to transform the economy; for all our problems, the labor movement can still draw on the energy, experience, intelligence, and resources of more than thirteen million members.

Then there are the peculiar features of the new economy — with lots of jobs available but with too many of them offering low pay, few benefits, little future, and no voice in decision making. Working people have good reason to be dissatisfied with their jobs; they're also confident that, as they often tell organizers, "If my boss fires me from this job, I'll be able to find another lousy job easily enough." In one indication of the large number of working people who want to organize, a blue-ribbon federal commission on labor relations recently found that one worker in three in private industry wants to join a union, compared with only the one in nine who currently belongs.

Recent experience shows that we can help working people

join together and improve wages and working conditions in their companies, communities, and entire industries.

One example of conditions improving industrywide is in building services, the historic heart of my home union, the Service Employees. By the middle of the 1980s, our members were threatened by far-reaching changes in the industry. Instead of employing their own janitorial staffs, building owners were contracting with nonunion building service companies. Part-time work was increasing, and wages were declining. Meanwhile, companies were leaving the heavily unionized cities and opening up their offices in largely nonunion suburbs and other new communities. Justice for Janitors originated with the union's successful campaign against Pittsburgh building owners' demands for pay cuts in their contract renegotiations in 1985.[2]

The strategy of Justice for Janitors was to build a mass movement, with workers making clear that they wanted union representation and winning "voluntary recognition" from employers. The campaigns addressed the special needs of an immigrant workforce, largely from Latin America. In many cities, the janitors' cause became a civil rights movement — and a cultural crusade.

After the victory in Pittsburgh, the next "crusade" came in Denver, in 1986. For nine months, union janitors blitzed the downtown office area, taking their message to nonunion janitors, picketing nonunion buildings, and getting arrested. Church officials, Latino leaders, and other community activists joined the cause. In less than a year, the union's membership among janitors in downtown Denver jumped from 30 to 70 percent. And janitors' wages rose by about ninety cents an hour. Soon, Justice for Janitors took root in San Diego. Once again, the union distributed bilingual materials, offered legal help to bilingual workers, and filed lawsuits on behalf of workers in state and federal courts.

The campaign has sent a clear message to major corporations: they cannot escape responsibility for the janitorial companies they hire. One of the most prominent targets was Apple Computer, which had been praised by *Working Mother* magazine as one of the most "family friendly" companies, and whose chief executive officer, at the time, John Sculley, had carefully cultivated a reputation as a progressive business leader. But Apple used a nonunion janitorial contractor, who paid low wages, with no benefits. The union called attention to the gap between Sculley's image and his actions. Activists took the message to computer shows, including Apple's Mac-World exhibitions. A group of five janitors held a hunger strike for five days in front of Apple headquarters in Cupertino, California. "The organizers did everything to make it appear that the problem was with Apple, not the janitorial service company," Sculley later recalled.

In the meantime, the union filed health and safety charges against Apple's janitorial firm, Shine Building Maintenance, and filed a lawsuit against it, charging wage and hour violations. Eventually, Apple felt the heat and saw the light. The janitorial firm signed a contract with the union. Other major companies in Silicon Valley followed suit and hired unionized cleaning companies.

Another battle in the campaign came in 1990 in Los Angeles, where two hundred janitors were on strike against International Service Systems (ISS), a huge Danish company. In June, the janitors and their supporters, including other union members and community activists, marched on the Century City office complex. There, they were attacked by two hundred Los Angeles police officers, in full riot gear and wielding batons. More than sixty demonstrators were hospitalized, with fractured skulls and broken bones. A pregnant woman was beaten in the stomach — and miscarried.

The janitors won worldwide sympathy for their courage in the face of the police riot. Soon, ISS agreed to bring twenty-five hundred janitors in Southern California under the union's master contract. Other leading companies, including Toyota and Mattel, extended union pay scales to 90 percent of the janitors in Los Angeles. And in 1995, the union won a countywide contract that raised janitors' pay to $6.80 an hour and gained them family medical benefits.

So far, Justice for Janitors has won some thirty-five thousand new members in Philadelphia, Hartford, Milwaukee, Los Angeles, San Diego, and other major cities. Its spirit is best expressed by Faustino Hernandez, a union janitor in Silicon Valley who has demonstrated and been arrested: "I do it to help other janitors, so that one day they will be able to have what I have now. Because of the union, there is now fairness on my job."

Another example of how working people can build their power and improve their lives is to be found in the textile industry in the South. In 1994, the Amalgamated Clothing and Textile Workers Union, now part of UNITE, won an NLRB election to represent some twenty-two hundred workers at the Tultex Corporation's factories in Martinsville, Virginia. Tultex has a pivotal position in the industry; it enjoys a large share of the market for sweatshirts and T-shirts, as well as items for the National Football League and the National Basketball Association. The company had been nonunion for fifty-seven years, and by organizing Tultex, the union strengthened its position in the textile industry in the Southeast.

Soon after the victory at the Martinsville plant, the union signed up another seven hundred employees at the company's plant in South Boston, Virginia. And it won some of the best contracts in the industry, with better pay and benefits and job security guarantees for workers who sew the garments — work that many companies contract out to low-wage companies overseas.

Just as important, having a union helps working people hold their heads a little higher. As Pamela (Spanky) Williams, a nineteen-year veteran at Tultex, said, "Now, it's a much better place to work. We work better. Supervisors will sit down and listen to you."

Union victories also have ripple effects, raising wages in entire communities as employers try to discourage organizing drives in their own companies. Soon after the Tultex workers won their election and their contract, factories in and around Martinsville raised wages for some ten thousand employees.

Because so many low-wage industries have settled in the South, that region is a special focus of our organizing efforts. In addition to clothing and textiles, another industry where working people are crying out for more dignity on the job is the poultry business. Maybe you remember the horrible fire that killed twenty-five workers at the Imperial Food Products Plant in Hamlet, North Carolina, on September 3, 1991. With grim irony, that was the day after Labor Day. The worst of the tragedy was that it didn't have to happen. When smoke spread from a fryer in the middle of the building, workers tried to escape from the burning building, but its doors were locked. Company officials later said the doors were locked to keep the workers from stealing chickens.

As someone who once served on the staff of the International Ladies Garment Workers Union, I was reminded by that infuriating fact of a story I'd heard from old-timers. In 1911, at the Triangle garment company in downtown Manhattan, 175 workers, mostly young women, died in a fire. There, too, the company had locked the doors, supposedly to prevent theft and possibly to keep out union organizers. As if to prove that there are no final victories for social justice, conditions in today's poultry industry resemble those in the worst sweatshops, past or present.

I'm always horrified when workers or organizers tell me about conditions on the "disassembly lines" in poultry plants. Workers stand shoulder to shoulder at the assembly line, wielding knives and boning chickens and cutting them apart at a frantic pace. After doing this hour after hour, day after day, they find their hands swollen or even crippled. Health and safety experts call this "repetitive motion syndrome." When workers talk about their problems, they're often asking for simple human dignity: bathroom breaks or a respite from the breakneck pace of their jobs.

The industry once consisted of hundreds of companies with thousands of plants across the country. Now, it's controlled by a handful of huge companies that have located in the South in search of low-wage labor. Of the 200,000 poultry workers, many are women, and large numbers are African Americans or recent immigrants from Latin America. Currently, only 20 percent belong to unions, but workers are organizing at an accelerating pace, with help from the Laborers union, the United Food and Commercial Workers, and the Retail, Wholesale, and Department Store Workers Union.[3]

At the Case Foods poultry plant in Morganton, North Carolina, some three hundred workers, primarily Guatemalan immigrants, walked off their jobs for four days in May 1995. The reason: three workers had been denied permission to go to the bathroom. In an election in July, the workers voted to join the Laborers union. Around the same time, more than a thousand workers at the Sanderson Farms poultry processing plants in Collins and Hazelhurst, Mississippi, also voted to join the Laborers.

For working Americans, these campaigns are a cause: the fight for fundamental dignity on the job. As Miguel Esquivel, a poultry worker in Morganton, said, "We need the protection of a union. Without it, the company can do what it wants to us."

Building Social Movements

Increasingly, unions will help working people build social movements. They'll bring together working people from many companies — sometimes from many occupations and industries. They'll reach out to other union members and our allies: civil rights groups, women's groups, churches and synagogues, community activists, environmentalists, and anyone and everyone who believes in social justice or simply wants to raise wages in the area.

A model for that effort is in Baltimore. It began with a leading organization in the African-American community, Baltimoreans United in Leadership Development (BUILD), which is sponsored by forty-five churches and is part of a national network of community organizations inspired by the legendary activist, the late Saul Alinsky. Since 1994, BUILD has been working with AFSCME, the union that represents most city government employees.[4]

The cause is a problem in communities around the country: the condition of workers who earn low wages for thankless jobs, from cleaning downtown office buildings and hotels to driving buses and serving food in the schools. Their plight raises basic issues of civic responsibility. Many work for contractors with the city and state governments. Others work in buildings in the Inner Harbor, a downtown urban renewal project that was sponsored by Baltimore's business community, with subsidies and loans from the city and federal governments.

Two decades ago, the city's African-American ministers supported the downtown development project in return for commitments from corporate leaders that many of the jobs would go to black workers. But, by the 1990s, as the ministers spoke with working people who regularly came to soup kitchens in their churches, it became clear that these were low-wage jobs with no benefits, not jobs with which working men and women could raise their families.

The ministers saw how the low-wage economy was tearing at the fabric of their communities. Parents who were holding down two jobs just to make ends meet — often during the days, the nights, and on weekends — were having trouble keeping an eye on their kids, taking part in PTAs and other community groups, maintaining their homes, or even joining in the life of their churches. As the Reverend Roger Gench, of Brown Memorial Park Avenue Presbyterian Church, said at a community meeting: "We must listen to our brothers and sisters who get off the bus every afternoon at Baltimore and Calvert — the people of the Third World workforce who come downtown every night to clean up after the First World workforce that's gone home."

A secretary at a mental health clinic, Christine Bubier, explained the problem even more vividly: "Here's my paycheck — it comes from the state. And here are my food stamps —

they come from the state, too. Why are they humiliating me like this? Why can't they put the money together in one paycheck?" While some pundits in Washington, D.C., draw distinctions between "economic" and "social" issues, the ministers knew better: the cause of much of the collapse in community life was the low wages that kept so many hardworking people away from their homes and their houses of worship. Moreover, the ministers understood that the cure for the problem was helping the workers organize for higher wages and better benefits. So they turned to AFSCME, the union representing the city employees whose jobs have increasingly been contracted out to private companies employing the low-wage workers BUILD is trying to organize. In fact, sometimes the employees of the private contractors are AFSCME members who were laid off from their city jobs, then hired — at lower wages — by the private contractors.

In May 1994, at a rally at Knox Presbyterian Church in East Baltimore, BUILD and AFSCME announced their partnership. Together, they founded the Solidarity Sponsoring Committee for low-wage workers throughout the city. It soon grew to several hundred members and was chartered as AFSCME Local 1711. Organizers continue to recruit members through the churches — or even by riding the buses that workers take to and from work, late at night and early in the morning. The Solidarity Sponsoring Committee's long-term goal is to organize employees of the cleaning companies and other firms that contract with government agencies and with office buildings and hotels in the downtown redevelopment area. With a union, these workers will be able to climb into the middle class, as million of American workers have done before them.

First, the BUILD/AFSCME alliance pursued another goal:

setting a living wage for workers employed by city contractors.

The movement found a pressure point: this time, they wouldn't support a bond issue for the Baltimore convention center — unless corporate leaders and the city government agreed to a "new social contract" for full-time jobs with living wages and a real future.

And they had a compelling case: low-wage workers like Christine Bubier were forced to draw on public subsidies, such as food stamps, to supplement their meager paychecks. Why not reward their hard work with a living wage so that they could support their families without public assistance? Armed with this argument, the alliance persuaded the city council to pass a "living wage" law in 1995. As of July 1, 1995, all workers employed by city contractors were to be paid at least $6.10 an hour. And within four years, their minimum wage is to jump to $7.70.

The victory not only raised workers' wages but lifted their spirits, as they saw what they could accomplish by working together. Blacka Wright, a part-time hotel housekeeper and a leader in the Solidarity Sponsoring Committee, said: "My dissatisfaction makes me angry, and my anger calms my fear and allows me to stand up and address these issues. If you're one person, they act like they don't see you. But, if you're two hundred or three hundred, they can't overlook it."

Meeting the Needs of the New Workforce

In 1993 and 1994, a blue-ribbon presidential commission took a look at our nation's labor laws and studied ways to make them more workable and fair. As part of their research, they commissioned a series of focus groups, in which working people talked about their problems on the job and how to solve them.

One session in Charlotte, North Carolina, included a sales representative, a database analyst, an insurance underwriter, and a bookkeeper. They said they didn't like unions — too many strikes, they thought. But as they kept talking, these employees admitted that they had problems, and they wanted their employers to pay attention to them. So they liked the idea of confronting management as a group. And they also wanted some support from outside experts — "consultants," as they called them.[5]

What these employees had thought up on their own sounds very much like something they said they didn't want — a union. Their discussion shows that there's great receptivity to organizing in every sector of society; after all, nobody ever thought that white-collar employees for private companies in the South were prime territory for unions. And it also shows that working people of all kinds will continue inventing and reinventing unionism to meet their own needs.

I've seen that all my life. As a youngster, when I attended meetings of the Transport Workers Union with my father, I marveled at how at home he felt. I shouldn't have been surprised: he and his union brothers had built an organization that met the needs and affirmed the attitudes of a workforce that was overwhelmingly male and blue collar. Later, as a union leader traveling across the country, I saw how groups as diverse as hospital workers, nurses, social workers, janitors, and librarians, to name just a few, all built organizations that they found comfortable, even welcoming.

Thanks to the news reports on the AFL-CIO's organizing efforts — and the anxieties fueled by corporate downsizings

— we're getting calls and letters from middle managers, computer programmers, and software writers, among the people in many professions.

As unions expand into new sectors of the workforce — from low-wage, largely immigrant workers to high-tech professionals — they'll find new ways to build organizations that meet their needs. For those of us already in the labor movement, our obligation is to help them organize themselves — and also to offer some models of organization, which they can choose among and, no doubt, improve upon.

A revitalized labor movement may reach out to workers in their occupations and professions, in the tradition of the old AFL. It will build mass movements to organize entire industries and be the core of a progressive political movement, in the tradition of the old CIO. And it will work closely with civil rights, women's rights, and community activists in the tradition of the 1960s and '70s.

Already, there are examples of unions working with groups of employees to create new kinds of organizations. For instance, at Harvard University, AFSCME has worked with what had been an independent organization of white-collar employees, the Harvard Union of Clerical and Technical Workers (HUCTW). After earlier, more conventional efforts at union organizing failed, HUCTW affiliated with AFSCME but retained its autonomy and its untraditional approach to organizing. Under the leadership of Kristine Rondeau, who had worked at the university as a medical research assistant, HUCTW avoided attacks on management, mass mailings and distributions of campaign literature, and other standard union tactics. Instead, as Rondeau explained, the emphasis was on winning the trust of individual workers through personal contact:

The union, through one or more of its representatives — whether that is staff or employee organizers — has to have a relationship with every person. There's nothing in this kind of organizing that is anything like electoral politics. Organizing workers is not about advertising. It's based on the belief that people change in relationships, not in isolation. Each person needs time to decide, a real connection to the union, and lots of information. But not just information — we call it "head and heart." That means that workers have to have some kind of emotional connection to the union as well as knowledge of it.[6]

Using the slogan "It's not anti-Harvard to be pro-union," HUCTW won an election in 1988 to represent the university's white-collar employees, most of whom are women with some college education. It has developed a remarkably participatory style of unionism that tries to work with management as a partner, not an adversary. More than a hundred employees throughout the university serve as elected union representatives, trying to solve their co-workers' problems by fashioning agreements between employees and their supervisors. In each of the university's schools and administrative offices, joint councils of employees and managers meet every two weeks in an effort to resolve problems concerning quality-of-worklife issues, such as scheduling, office space assignments, and health and safety problems.[7]

What's happening at Harvard is one of a growing number of efforts by national unions to work with the independent associations that working people, particularly clerical and professional employees, have formed to meet their needs on the job. In 1981, the Service Employees joined forces with 9 to 5, the National Organization of Working Women, to launch a national organizing drive aimed at clerical workers.

A new nationwide local was chartered — District 925 — which has grown to 12,000 members.

Using the AFL-CIO's Union Privilege Benefit Program, several unions offer "associate memberships" to workers who are not covered under collective bargaining agreements. Usually, these members receive low-cost services, such as a union-sponsored credit card, legal assistance, mortgage and personal loans, insurance, and other goods and services. The union may also provide information about issues in their occupations and industries and, sometimes, advice or representation in individual problems on the job.

The AFT, for instance, has organized thousands of teachers as associate members in those states, such as Louisiana and Texas, which do not have collective-bargaining laws. The CWA has experimented with new forms of organizing for workers in the communications and high-tech industries. And the AFL-CIO has established the California Immigrant Workers Association to help immigrant workers get legal advice, education and training, and other services, and has formed associate member programs in Montana, El Paso, and Cincinnati.

New forms of organization may be especially appropriate for the fast-growing contingent workforce, which does not have regular employers and is not covered under national labor legislation but faces severe problems at work.

Another way that a revitalized labor movement will meet the needs of the new workforce is by being a source of job training and retraining and information on employment opportunities. At the AFL-CIO, we're going to encourage unions to build on what many are already doing.[8] For instance, UNITE runs "justice centers" for immigrant workers in New York, Los Angeles, and other cities. In Los Angeles, where the union offers legal assistance, it also provides language and citizenship classes, as well as training and job advice.

The UAW works with Ford, Chrysler, and General Motors on training programs that help workers further their education and improve their skills. These are among the largest programs of this kind anywhere in the world.

And nearly 40 percent of active AT&T employees participate in education and training programs cosponsored with the CWA and IBEW. The services include career assessment and planning, prepaid college tuition, basic skills upgrading, job search assistance, and stress management techniques.

SEIU and AFSCME sponsor career ladder programs that help workers in state and local governments and health-care facilities move up from low-wage jobs to skilled positions, such as registered nurses and social workers. In Illinois, AFSCME's Upward Mobility Program has helped more than a thousand state employees reach their targeted jobs by following personal education plans, devised through one-on-one counseling.

Meanwhile, there's much that unions can learn from the oldest "learning by doing" programs of all — the apprenticeship training in the building trades. As more skilled workers — from nurses and engineers to software writers and computer professionals — organize themselves, they may adapt a time-honored model of unionism: defining the skills a profession requires, training and certifying newcomers, and providing skilled employees to employers.

At the AFL-CIO, we're committed to helping these working people meet their own needs; we don't want to impose a one-size-fits-all pattern of unionism on every working person in every occupation in every sector of the economy.

That is one reason that I've created the Committee 2000, to

take a thorough top-to-bottom look at unionism in America. We're taking nothing for granted — from the structure dating from the 1930s, where unions are based in companies and industries, to the view that our most important function is to bargain and enforce contracts. Sure, I expect that most unions will continue to fit this pattern, but I also hope we'll find new ways to help the new workforce meet new needs.

If you have ideas about how unions can transform themselves to meet your needs and the needs of your co-workers, then write to me at the AFL-CIO, 815 16th Street N.W., Washington, D.C. 20005. No kidding; we need all the ideas we can get.

Fighting to Win

A revitalized labor movement will offer working Americans a way to win better pay, benefits, conditions, and opportunities — even in the face of attacks from powerful corporations. The challenge is to find ways for working people to support each other in their struggles and to plan sophisticated strategies to use media coverage, political clout, community organizing, international support, and even pressure from investors and major customers to persuade employers to come to terms. That's why the AFL-CIO is creating an Office of Strategic Approaches; it will help working people find ways to fight and win.

After two decades during which working Americans took it on the chin, there are signs that they can prevail in contract battles, as seen in two struggles that were under way when I became president of the AFL-CIO.

One of the first things I did as president of the federation was march with striking Boeing workers in Everett, Washington, in November 1995. More than thirty-two thousand Machinists union members in Washington, Oregon, and Kansas held out for sixty-nine days against Boeing, the world's largest producer of commercial jet aircraft. They were up against the company's record of aggressively outsourcing work to outside contractors in the United States and overseas, espcially China, Japan, and other nations in the Pacific Rim. On top of that, management proposed only meager pay increases, at the same time as it sought cuts in retiree benefits. It also tried to get contract language that would let outside vendors do production and tooling work in Boeing shops. And, to add insult to injury, in the middle of the strike, the company announced that the Boeing chairman and CEO, Frank Schrontz, and four other top executives were eligible for a total of some $2.5 million in bonuses.

In the face of all this, Boeing workers stood fast and eventually won unprecedented job security protections, improved health and pension benefits, and substantial pay raises and bonuses. One enthusiastic union member called it a "slam-dunk."[9]

Just a few days before marching against Boeing, I addressed a rally in Baltimore's Camden Yards stadium, supporting the employees of the nation's second-largest telecommunications company, Bell Atlantic. One of the regional Bell companies that spun off from AT&T during the 1980s, Bell Atlantic was flush with cash, having earned profits of $1.4 billion on revenues of $13.8 billion in 1994. Still, the company was refusing to follow the pattern the CWA had established in negotiations with the other regional companies. Instead, it was trying to subcontract workers' jobs and cut retirees' benefits.

Rather than strike, CWA members were waging a sophisticated corporate campaign, embarrassing Bell Atlantic with its consumers and shareholders. At a cost of approximately $7 million — one week's worth of strike benefits — the CWA ran messages on TV, the radio, and in the newspapers in the company's service area: Pennsylvania, New Jersey, Delaware, Maryland, Virginia, West Virginia, and Washington, D.C. The messages hit hard at Bell Atlantic as a profitable company forcing loyal retirees to pay for health care and farming out work to subcontractors who offered inferior services. One especially effective TV spot featured Larry, a bumbling repairman for a subcontractor. This fellow shows up late at a family's home and then bungles the repair job. All in all, the TV spots alone reached an estimated 5.8 million people — and must have had Bell Atlantic executives popping antacid tablets.

Meanwhile, CWA members mobilized in their workplaces and communities. While there were no work stoppages, Bell Atlantic employees frequently held "work to rule" protests — where they followed their job descriptions to the letter, and no more — and refused overtime assignments. And workers took their message to the public, leafleting consumers and wearing T-shirts with the slogan, "We won't be road kill on the information superhighway." After five months of bad publicity and hard bargaining, Bell Atlantic settled with the CWA, agreeing to a contract with substantial pay increases, improved health and pension benefits, and protections against subcontracting.

Recent experience reveals two other ways that working people can build the strength to prevail against giant corporations: by arranging mergers of unions in similar industries and by making common cause with working people in other countries.

I've already explained how working people in the garment and textile industries have a powerful ally in their efforts to organize for better pay and conditions, thanks to the recent merger of the International Ladies Garment Workers Union and the Amalgamated Clothing and Textile Workers Union into the new union UNITE.

Similarly, within a few years there will be a powerful new union representing more than two million workers in such industries as automobiles, steel, aerospace, machine tools, and farm equipment. That's because the United Auto Workers, Machinists, and Steelworkers — each of them a strong union with its own proud traditions — have decided to merge by the year 2000, offering the opportunity for working people to deal with giant multinational corporations like General Motors, Boeing, and USX (formerly U.S. Steel) from a position of unprecedented strength. This is a tribute to the vision and decisiveness of UAW President Steve Yokich, Machinists President George Kourpias, and Steelworkers President George Becker, who, at a meeting in 1995, came to the conclusion that the merger was necessary. Earlier that year, the United Rubber Workers merged with the Steelworkers.

Working Americans can continue to build their strength — especially when they're up against huge transnational companies — by reaching out to working people around the world. The AFL-CIO will be a central source of information on global corporate organizations and will help unions in the United States work in a coordinated way with unions from other countries. It will also keep an eye on the work of such powerful international institutions as the World Bank and the International Monetary Fund, and assess the impact of trade agreements, like NAFTA and GATT, on American workers. But what's most important is strengthening the impulse

among working people to reach across national borders to
help one another in the efforts to win higher pay, better
conditions, and simple justice.

An encouraging example of international solidarity has
emerged under surprising circumstances. In 1994, the CWA
signed up a majority of the employees at La Conexión Familiar, a unit of the telecommunications company Sprint that
provides long-distance services for Spanish-speaking customers. Rather than allow the employees to vote on whether to be
represented by the union, Sprint closed down the service —
and the NLRB upheld the CWA's claim that Sprint had engaged in unfair labor practices. CWA President Morton Bahr
then tried an innovative tactic. He worked with the Mexican
telephone workers' union, and it filed a complaint under
NAFTA charging that, by failing to enforce its own labor
laws, the U.S. government had engaged in an unfair trade
practice that put Mexican workers at an unfair disadvantage.

Now, don't get me wrong: I still think NAFTA does more
harm than good for working people in the United States and
Mexico. But like the biblical David who picked up stones and
hurled them at Goliath, working people should, I think, use
any weapon at their disposal, including the labor protection
language that the Clinton administration did succeed in in-
serting into NAFTA (which made the agreement better than
the treaty the Bush administration had negotiated, though
still not good enough).

Most of all, it's encouraging whenever workers in the
U.S.A. are able to join with workers from other countries in
an effort to win some justice from multinational corporations. Our labor movement will try to do that more often in
the years ahead, as we grapple with global employers in a
global economy.

Winning a Voice in Decision Making

As we build our strength — and prove that we can exert pressure on corporate America — working people will reach out to management from a position of power and seek a greater voice in making decisions that affect us.

A revitalized labor movement will give voice to working people's yearning for some say in how they spend their lives on the job — and for the sense of pride and purpose that comes with making better products and providing better services.

A new movement of working people should also understand that we can no longer afford the luxury of pretending that productivity, quality, and competitiveness are not our business. They are our business, our jobs, and our paychecks.

Too many workers — including my own brother, Jim, who left IBM just before he would have been "downsized" — have suffered because of failed and foolish management policies. We need to win a share of power in decision making so that we can improve the products we make and the services we deliver — and, often, save our bosses from themselves.

I'm talking about a partnership of equals. Labor and management will always have adversarial roles, and that relationship is part of a healthy balance of power in our democracy, just like the relationship between the news media and public officials, or between prosecutors and defense attorneys.

But, just as Perry Mason and Hamilton Burger respected each other and shared a passion for justice, labor and management should be able to work out their differences and pursue their common goals in an atmosphere of mutual respect.

148   *America Needs a Raise*

We have got to find ways for the voice of working people to be heard in making decisions that they often understand better than their bosses. After all, the people who build automobiles frequently have the best ideas about how to make better cars; nurses care deeply about improving health care; and teachers understand the realities of education better than ivory-tower theoreticians who haven't been in a classroom since blackboards turned green.

Given the choice, almost every worker and every union would rather have a partnership with employers, one that offers them the opportunity to improve quality and share in the rewards of success. The problem is that we rarely get that chance.

Even our harshest critics have a hard time pointing to recent examples of employers offering partnerships to their employees and their unions — and being turned down. But there are far too many examples of companies — from Eastern Airlines and Caterpillar to Xerox, AT&T, and Boeing — where workers gladly cooperated with their employers, only to see the existing management or its successors change course without warning and begin massive layoffs or demand severe cuts in pay and benefits. These experiences, as well as a memory of the "give-backs" in pay and benefits during the 1970s and 1980s, have created an environment of distrust in many industries and companies that will take much time and effort to dispel.

So, in the near future, we will devote most of our energy to building a stronger, smarter labor movement. Then we'll be in a position to offer management a new social contract by which we will share power, profits, and prosperity. We prefer cooperation to conflict, but we must be prepared for both; ultimately, the choice is management's to make. Throughout

the economy, there are already examples of partnerships between employers and employees that are beneficial to both
sides and that improve quality and competitiveness. These
examples offer a glimpse of what we can accomplish together
with the new social contract we seek.

On a trip to Pennsylvania in October 1995, during my
campaign for president of the AFL-CIO, I saw both sides
of labor-management relations — cooperation and confron-
tation.

First, I visited the USX Corporation's Mon Valley Works,
along with the United Steelworkers president, George Becker.
I was impressed by how well workers and management are
working together. A labor-management committee meets
regularly to discuss how to solve shop-floor problems and
improve the quality of the steel they're producing. The plant
also has an educational program that helps workers sharpen
their skills, from mathematics and computer literacy to rewir-
ing their homes and repairing videocassette recorders. Meanwhile, the union contract provides that the Steelworkers can
recommend a candidate for the USX board of directors who
will represent the employees' interests as stakeholders of the
corporation. Currently, former labor secretary Ray Marshall
serves in that position.

Elsewhere in the steel industry, which once was the scene
of bitter battles, Inland Steel and National Steel have reached
historic agreements with the union to share productivity gains
with their workers.[10]

But, later that day, I was reminded once again that many
companies refuse to respect workers' rights. At the parking
lot at a nearby Sears, at a demonstration of 300 union members, their families, and supporters, I spoke from the back of
a pickup truck. We were urging customers not to buy tires

made by Bridgestone-Firestone, which had forced its employees to strike by taking away traditional holiday and seniority protections. With us was Tammy Lee, who had worked at the Bridgestone-Firestone factory in Noblesville, Indiana. Like many of her co-workers, she had been replaced by the company to which she had loyally given many years of her life.

At the world's largest apparel manufacturer, Levi Strauss, management and the union, UNITE, have joined in a historic partnership to give the workers a real voice in shaping strategy. At the corporate level, union and management officials meet regularly to discuss companywide issues and set strategies for competing on the world market.[11] In the plants, managers and workers meet together regularly to plan the pace of work, devise bonus awards for employees who have done outstanding work, and design programs to train employees for several jobs. Under this cross-training system, workers get a sense of the big picture and are spared the monotony and physical hazards of doing the same tasks over and over.

And in the auto industry, one of the most successful new cars — Chrysler's subcompact Neon — was built and developed with worker involvement from Day One. At the Chrysler plant in Belvidere, Illinois, the UAW and management resolved past problems and have established a cooperative working relationship. Now, management officials, production workers, designers, and engineers sit down together and decide how to build better cars. Workers' power is a big part of the process. All in all, there are 125 operations where workers can shut down the production line to correct quality problems. In one example of how UAW members offered ideas on how to do their jobs better, workers in the paint shop created an antichip formula that they are applying to the fenders and the hood of the cars to protect the finish.

In the federal government, the American Federation of Government Employees, under the leadership of its president, John Sturdivant, is working with the Clinton administration in an effort to "reinvent government," by making it more efficient and effective. Similar stories are taking place in state and local governments. In Massachusetts in 1993, SEIU and AFSCME locals got together when Governor Weld planned to contract out work from the Highway Department in October 1993, a move that would have wiped out 424 maintenance workers' jobs. So the unions submitted bids on all seven areas marked for privatization, drawing on the workers' experience to suggest ways to improve efficiency. They won three highway maintenance contracts for roads and bridges in southeastern Massachusetts. This saved 264 union jobs, and it saved the taxpayers more than $7.8 million in operating costs.

Similarly, in upstate New York, Saratoga County government and AFSCME worked together to find ways to improve highway maintenance and snow removal. Frontline workers were given the chance to make such decisions as setting priorities, defining tasks, and revamping schedules. One example of the changes that saved the taxpayers $100,000 was the workers' decision to redeploy themselves to daytime repair projects, instead of maintaining snow crews in place every night, whether it snowed or not. This more than paid for the overtime needed to plow the streets faster on the nights when it actually did snow.

Teachers, too, are taking greater responsibility for the quality of their work. AFT locals in Rochester, New York, and in Cincinnati and Toledo have designed peer review programs to monitor and improve the quality of teaching. In New York City, the union has worked with the school district to reor-

ganize schools that showed poor performance. AFT President
Al Shanker and teachers' unions in many cities across the
country are taking the lead in proposing reforms that will
raise the standards for students' achievement and behavior.

Restoring Community

Finally, a revitalized labor movement can help working Americans restore their sense of community.

As people work longer hours and hardly have the time to
meet their neighbors, the workplace is becoming the true
community for many people. Individuals who would never
live together, play together, or pray together do work alongside one another. And when they join together in unions, they
have the chance to learn that they share common interests
and, often, common values.

I don't mean to be misty-eyed. I've seen too much fear and
prejudice and even raw hatred to suggest that, just because
they belong to the same union, blacks and whites, Latinos
and Asians, evangelicals and agnostics, are all going to march
off into the sunset together, carrying picket signs and singing
folk songs. But there are some practical reasons why unions
must try to bring working people together — and why working people will usually respond to these appeals.

For all the discrimination in hiring and promotions, few
workplaces are entirely homogeneous. Men as well as women
work as clerical employees. African Americans, Asian Americans, Latinos, and, yes, Anglo whites as well, work alongside
one another in garment districts. And every one of the racial
categories I just mentioned includes a rich diversity of heri-
tages — black Americans, people from the Caribbean, China,

Korea, Vietnam, Thailand, Mexico, El Salvador, Guatemala, Russia, Poland, Italy, Greece, and, if there's anyone from Ireland, we're sure to find each other.

The point is: to have any power in the workplace, a union has to find a way to bring together all workers. That means putting aside anything divisive or offensive and making appeals that are unifying. Once working people understand that the only way to protect their paychecks is to stand together, they're likely to look past their prejudices to their shared goals.

That helps to explain why the best union leaders have usually been gifted ethnic diplomats. Walter Reuther and A. Philip Randolph, Sidney Hillman and Cesar Chavez — all were honored in their time for addressing working people from different backgrounds and helping them see what they had in common.

Out there today are organizers whose names you haven't heard — women and men who can talk to high school dropouts and college graduates, street sweepers and software writers, and have them nodding in agreement. The point is that successful organizers and union leaders must find ways to emphasize the things that unite us, not divide us.

That's also why, when the hate mongers come to town, some of the first people who get called in to help beat back the bigots are leaders of local unions. After all, when it comes to pulling people together, they have more experience than anyone except the clergy. For instance, starting in 1993, the good people of Billings, Montana, were alarmed when the Ku Klux Klan and other hate groups started harassing blacks, Jews, Native Americans, and gays.[12]

Members of the Laborers and Painters unions led a movement to stop the white supremacists from getting a toehold in town. Randy Seimers, an active member of the Laborers, attended a community meeting and heard about the overturning of tombstones in a Jewish cemetery. He got the Billings Labor Council to pass a resolution against hate crimes and volunteered to help the local police protect people at anti-hate rallies.

Not long afterward, vandals spray-painted swastikas on a Native American woman's home. Sarah Anthony of the Billings Coalition for Human Rights told Bob Maxwell, business agent for the Painters local, of the incident. "As soon as I heard about the acts of vandalism, I offered the services of our local," Maxwell said later. More than thirty union painters helped to repaint the house, cheered on by some hundred townspeople.

That spirit of community and solidarity is what a stronger, more active union movement can offer America as an antidote not only to bigotry and violence but to the sense that there is nothing we can do to make things better.

Making "Hope and History Rhyme"

I want to end this book as I began, with four simple words that say a lot about what's on working people's minds: America needs a raise.

So let's say that, just like most folks who work for a living, you too need a raise. Imagine that you walk into your boss's office and ask for a raise. No matter how valuable you are, he or she could ignore you. So imagine next that everyone you work with walked into your boss's office and asked for a raise. This time, he or she would have a hard time ignoring all of you — from the production workers to the clerical employees, the receptionists, and the accountants.

Chances are that now your boss just might give every one of you a raise. And chances are that — all the employees, together — would have a little more leverage over your employer in the future. You could use that leverage to win other improvements in your jobs — perhaps a better system for training and promoting people, or even some say in how you all could do your work better.

On a larger scale, that's what the movement I envision is about: offering working Americans a stronger voice so that together they can improve their lives and livelihoods, their companies, their communities, and their country.

Most of all, this movement is about building big changes out of seemingly small victories. Winning a pay raise for women and men who clean office buildings at night. Improving health coverage for telephone operators and their children. Bargaining better pensions for carpenters and clothing workers. And offering social workers the opportunity to control their caseload sizes and teachers the opportunity to control their class sizes, so they all can do their jobs better.

But as we win these victories, we'll be achieving greater goals as well. We'll make work more attractive than welfare and lift the working poor into the middle class. We'll win the middle class more security; when people have less reason to fear the future, there will be less meanness in our society and our politics. We'll ease some of the inequality in wages and wealth between the people who do America's work and the people who profit from their work. And by achieving these victories, we will help to make Americans more confident in their own lives and more comfortable with each other.

More than that, we'll restore the sense that our society has respect for all work and offers dignity for all workers. We'll put new life into old-fashioned virtues, such as pride in our work and loyalty to our co-workers and our company. And we'll offer working people the opportunity to win some power over how they do their jobs and then use that power for a purpose: to build better cars and computers, to do the best job possible of caring for the sick, teaching the children, and counseling those who have fallen on hard times. All this will help to make our families more secure, our companies more successful, our economy more prosperous, and our society more stable and cohesive.

The movement that we seek to build is both a means to these ends and an accomplishment in itself. As I like to remind leaders of our movement, labor unions still have more than thirteen million members around the country. If we mobilized only 2 percent of those members, we would have an army of more than a quarter million Americans from every background and walk of life, ready to devote their energies to social justice and community service.

Then imagine if we mobilized a larger share of a larger movement. Imagine if half a million — or, better yet, a million — working men and women devoted some of their spare time to organizing exploited workers, raising their wages, and helping them support their families without food stamps. Or registering voters and electing candidates committed to health care for every working family, not to subsidies for wealthy corporations. Or mobilizing their own co-workers to pressure their employers to let the employees use their hard-earned knowledge to find ways to improve the company's products. Or training young people to become skilled electricians or dedicated teachers. Or organizing communities from Billings to the Bronx to answer the voices of hatred and hopelessness.

That is what a larger, stronger, more active labor movement can mean for America. That's the vision that keeps so many of us going: that we can reshape the world in which we live in the image of our dreams and values.

On a wonderful trip to a troubled place, I found myself thinking about how people don't have to accept things as they are and always have been.

President Clinton asked me to join him on his journey of peacemaking all across Ireland. In a delicious irony, I had the honor of traveling with the president in the country my father and mother had left by traveling by ship in something close to steerage.

One of our first stops in Northern Ireland was at the Mackie Engineering Works in Belfast. For years, Catholics had been shunted into the worst jobs in that factory, much like black workers in the United States. Now, Catholics and Protestants work together on the shop floor, and labor and management cooperate at the bargaining table. Productivity, profits, and wages are all rising, and the company is investing in new equipment and new jobs.

The lesson is clear: when there is dignity for everyone, everyone wins. And even in the most divided and despairing societies, social justice can begin in the workplace.

On that trip, President Clinton met the Nobel Prize–winning poet Seamus Heaney, who once wrote these words: "History says don't hope on this side of the grave. But, once in a lifetime, the longed-for tidal wave of justice can rise up — and hope and history rhyme."

Soon, in answer to the assault on our jobs and wages, working men and women will once again "rise up" like "the longed-for tidal wave of justice." And we can make it one of those rare moments when "hope and history rhyme."

Notes

1. It Doesn't Have to Be This Way

1. For more about Albert ("Chain Saw") Dunlap's career, see Allan Sloan, "The Hit Men," *Newsweek,* Feb. 26, 1996, pp. 44–48.
2. For an excellent presentation of the progressive social teaching of the Catholic church, as well as the memoirs of our nation's leading labor priest, see Msgr. George C. Higgins, with William Bole, *Organized Labor and the Church: Reflections of a "Labor Priest,"* Mahwah, N.J.: Paulist Press, 1993.
3. Colin L. Powell with Joseph Persico, *My American Journey,* New York: Random House, 1995, p. 607.
4. See Brother C. Justin, F.S.C., head of the Labor-Management Department at Manhattan College, with Amedeo Giorgi, Ph.D., Psychology Department, Manhattan College, and Thomas J. Wright, P.E., Labor-Management Department, Manhattan College, *The Impact of Automation on the Elevator Service Industry on Manhattan Island.* Paper published in 1962.
5. The quote from the Los Angeles nurse is from *Nurses: On the Front Line of Patient Care,* Service Employees International Union, 1991, p. 21.
6. For historical information about the SEIU cited here and throughout this book, see Tom Beadling, Pat Cooper, Grace Palladino, and Peter Pieragostini, *A Need for Valor* (SEIU, 1984).
7. See Peter Pieragostini, "A Study in Horror," *Union,* magazine of the Service Employees International Union, March–April 1995, pp. 15–18. The AFL-CIO report considered state inspection records and Beverly's internal quality reviews.

8. "Worker Protection: Federal Contractors and Violations of Labor Law," Report to the Honorable Paul Simon, U.S. Senate by the U.S. General Accounting Office, Oct. 1995.

9. For coverage of the Justice for Janitors campaign, see Tom Beadling, Pat Cooper, Grace Palladino, and Peter Pieragostini, *A Need for Valor,* pp. 81–84.

2. *Downsized Dreams*

1. Facts about Eddie Neace from David Elsila, "Toward a More Perfect Union, Young Workers Join Together to Make a Better Future," UAW Solidarity, Jan.–Feb. 1996, pp. 8–10, and from an interview with research assistant Carter Wright in March 1996.

2. For statistics on wages, see Aaron Bernstein, "The Wage Squeeze," *Business Week,* July 17, 1995, pp. 54–62; Lawrence Mishel and Jared Bernstein, *The State of Working America, 1994–95,* Economic Policy Institute, Armonk, N.Y.: M. E. Sharpe, 1994; and "America Needs a Raise," a paper by the AFL-CIO Department of Economic Research, Feb. 1996.

3. Susan Sheehan, "Ain't No Middle Class," *The New Yorker,* Dec. 11, 1995, pp. 82–93.

4. For coverage of "contingent" workers, see Jane Bryant Quinn, *Newsweek,* Sept. 23, 1991, p. 41, and Sara Collins, "The New Migrant Workers," *U.S. News & World Report,* July 4, 1994, pp. 53–55.

5. Stanley B. Greenberg, Greenberg Research, *The Economy Project.* Survey prepared for the AFL-CIO and the Service Employees International Union, 1996, p. 35.

6. For more on productivity and wages, see David Obey and Scott Lilly, "Who Is Downsizing the American Dream?" Democratic Policy Committee Staff Report, March 11, 1996, p. 7.

7. Stanley B. Greenberg, Greenberg Research, *The Economy Project,* p. 35.

8. Commission on the Future of Worker-Management Relations (Dunlop Commission), Vol. 1: Fact-Finding Report, U.S. Government Printing Office, May 1994, p. 92.

9. For figures on the decline of unionism and its impact on living

standards, see Aaron Bernstein, "Why America Needs Unions but Not the Kind It Has Now," *Business Week,* May 23, 1994, pp. 70–82.

10. Steven V. Roberts, "Workers Take It on the Chin," *U.S. News & World Report,* Jan. 22, 1996.

11. For more about executive pay, see David Obey and Scott Lilly, "Who Is Downsizing the American Dream?" Democratic Policy Committee Staff Report, March 11, 1996, pp. 15–17.

12. For the section from the IBM personnel manual, see Joseph Nocera, "Living with Layoffs," *Fortune,* April 1, 1996, p. 69.

13. Louis Uchitelle, N. R. Kleinfeld, Sara Rimer, et al., "The Downsizing of America," a seven-part series, *The New York Times,* March 3–9, 1996.

14. For coverage of new corporate pay plans at Mobil and elsewhere, see Aaron Bernstein, "The Wage Squeeze," *Business Week,* July 17, 1995, pp. 57 and 60.

15. Stanley B. Greenberg, Greenberg Research, *The Economy Project,* p. 7.

16. Ibid.

17. Robert D. Putnam, "The Strange Disappearance of Civic America," *The American Prospect,* winter 1996, pp. 34–50.

18. For statistics and stories from working women, see *Working Women Count: A Report to the Nation,* Women's Bureau, U.S. Department of Labor, U.S. Government Printing Office, 1994, and "Voices of Working Women Time Capsule," in honor of the seventy-fifth anniversary of the Women's Bureau and the working women of America, presented to President Bill Clinton, the White House, May 19, 1995.

19. Ibid.

20. Ibid.

21. For the Celinda Lake quote, see Steven V. Roberts, "Workers Take It on the Chin," *U.S. News & World Report,* January 22, 1996.

22. For quote from North Carolina parent, see David Obey and Scott Lilly, "Who is Downsizing the American Dream?" Democratic Policy Committee Staff Report, March 11, 1996, p. 1.

23. Robert D. Putnam, "The Strange Disappearance of Civic America," *The American Prospect,* winter 1996, pp. 34–50.

24. "Job Anxiety Cuts Deeply in Illinois," Chicago Tribune Staff, *The Chicago Tribune*, March 17, 1996, pp. 1 and 10.

25. For quote from retired laborer in Philadelphia, see Peter D. Hart Research Associates, AFL-CIO Wages Focus Group, Blue-Collar Men, Philadelphia, 1996.

26. For quote from white-collar woman in Baltimore, see Peter D. Hart Research Associates, AFL-CIO Wages Focus Group, White-Collar Women, Philadelphia, 1996.

27. Joann S. Lublin, "Walking Wounded: Survivors of Layoffs Battle Angst, Anger, Hurting Productivity," *The Wall Street Journal*, Dec. 6, 1993, p. 1.

28. For coverage of Cal Ripken's loyalty to his teammates and fans, see Mark Hyman, "Ripken Won't Play Despite Union Offer," *The Baltimore Sun*, Dec. 29, 1994, p. 1C; Jerry Heaster, "Ripken Is True to the Cause," *The Kansas City Star*, Jan. 4, 1995, p. B1; Peter Schmuck, "Fehr Vows Ripken Support," *The Baltimore Sun*, March 16, 1995, p. 1D; Jerry Heaster, "America Honors Its Work Ethic," *The Kansas City Star*, Sept. 8, 1995, p. B1.

29. For coverage of Aaron Feuerstein, see Tom Witkowski, "The Glow from a Fire," *Time*, Jan. 8, 1996, p. 49.

30. For the results of this survey, see "Portrait of an Anxious Public," *Business Week*, March 13, 1995, p. 80.

3. Who's Doing It to You?

1. Political analyst Ruy Teixeira has written insightfully about the "stories" Americans accept as explanations for stagnant living standards. See his afterword, "Political Reality," in *Reclaiming Prosperity: A Blueprint for Progressive Economic Reform*, Economic Policy Institute, Armonk, N.Y.: M. E. Sharpe, Inc., 1995, pp. 321–335.

2. For the results of this survey, see "Portrait of an Anxious Public," *Business Week*, March 13, 1995, p. 80.

3. For figures on changes in tax burdens, see Lawrence Mishel and David M. Frankel, *The State of Working America, 1990–1991*, Economic Policy Institute, Armonk, N.Y.: M. E. Sharpe, Inc., 1990, pp. 55, 69.

4. For figures on low wages overseas, see Richard Rothstein, "The Global Hiring Hall," *The American Prospect,* spring 1994, pp. 54–62.

5. For the story of how Walter Reuther tried to persuade the big three auto companies to build small cars, see David Halberstam, *The Reckoning,* New York: William Morrow and Company, 1986, p. 346.

6. For figures on corporate PACs, see Edward Zuckerman, *Almanac of Federal PACs: 1990,* Washington, D.C.: Amward Publications, 1990, especially p. 595.

7. See Thomas Byrne Edsall, *The New Politics of Inequality,* New York: W. W. Norton, 1984, pp. 128–129.

8. For coverage of Douglas Fraser's withdrawal from the Labor Management Committee, see Philip Shabecoff, "Auto Union Head Protests Role of Business, Quits Carter Panel," *The New York Times,* July 23, 1978, sec. III, p. 2.

9. For the quote about Federal Reserve policies, see David Obey and Scott Lilly, "Who Is Downsizing the American Dream?" Democratic Policy Committee Staff Report, March 11, 1996, p. 31.

10. Thomas R. Donahue, Secretary-Treasurer, AFL-CIO, Statement before the Senate Labor and Human Resources Committee, 1981.

11. Robert B. Reich, *The Work of Nations,* New York: Alfred A. Knopf, 1991, p. 119.

12. For coverage of Mobil and other corporate pay plans, see Aaron Bernstein, "The Wage Squeeze," *Business Week,* July 17, 1995, pp. 57, 60.

13. John Judis, "Why Your Wages Keep Falling," *The New Republic,* Feb. 14, 1994, pp. 26–29.

14. For statistics on anti-union consultants, see David Kusnet, "A Dirty Business," *Commonweal,* Feb. 24, 1989, pp. 107–108.

15. This account of the failure of the NLRB election process draws upon Richard Rothstein, "Labor Law Reform 1: New Bargain or No Bargain," *The American Prospect,* summer 1993, pp. 32–48, and Steven Lerner, "Let's Get Moving: Labor's Survival Depends on Organizing Industry-wide for Justice and Power," *Labor Research Review 18,* Chicago: Midwest Center for Labor

Research, 1991. Rothstein was on the staff of the Amalgamated Clothing and Textile Workers Union for 15 years and was organizing director of the J. P. Stevens campaign. Lerner was director of the Building Service Division of SEIU and a leading strategist for the Justice for Janitors campaign.

16. For estimate of workers fired during organizing campaigns, see Thomas Geoghegan, *Which Side Are You On? Trying to Be for Labor When It's Flat on Its Back,* New York: Farrar, Straus & Giroux, 1991, p. 234.

17. See Steve Lerner, "Let's Get Moving! Organizing for the 90s," *Labor Research Review 18,* fall/winter 1991/92, Chicago: Midwest Center for Labor Research, 1991.

18. For statement by department store employee Judy Ray, see Commission on the Future of Worker-Management Relations (Dunlop Commission), Vol. 1: Fact-Finding Report, U.S. Government Printing Office, May 1994, p. 89.

19. For statement by Highland Yarn Mills worker Florence Hill, see ibid., pp. 89 and 90.

20. This is from "Being Heard," a report prepared for the AFL-CIO by Greer, Margolis, Mitchell, Burns, and Associates, Inc., with Research and Findings by Peter D. Hart Research, March 21, 1994.

21. For coverage of the campaign for president of the AFL-CIO and the 1995 AFL-CIO Convention, see Harold Meyerson, "Bomb Throwers of Bal Harbour," *LA Weekly,* March 10–16, 1995; Frank Swoboda, "Kirkland Will Leave AFL-CIO," *The Washington Post,* June 13, 1995, p. A1; John B. Judis, "Sweeney Agonistes: Can Anybody Save the AFL-CIO?" *The New Republic,* Aug. 21 and 28, 1995, pp. 23–27; John Greenwald, "The Battle to Revive the Unions," *Time,* Oct. 30, 1995, pp. 64–66.

4. People Politics

1. A notable exception was *Business Week,* which provided excellent coverage of the issue of stagnant wages during 1995, including a cover story on the problem.

2. Garin-Hart Strategic Research, "How It Can't Happen Here Almost Happened in Louisiana: A Study of the David Duke Phe-

nomenon in the 1990 Senate Race." Paper prepared for the Center for National Policy, March 1991.

3. See Teixiera's articles and papers on swing voters, including "What Kind of New Democrat Should Bill Clinton Be: Understanding the 1994 Election Results," Economic Policy Institute, Dec. 16, 1994.

4. Peter D. Hart Research Associates, Focus Group, Cleveland Men, Feb. 6, 1996.

5. Peter D. Hart Research Associates, Focus Group, Cleveland Women, Feb. 6, 1996.

6. For figures about PAC donations, see Julie Kosterlitz, "Laboring Uphill," *National Journal*, March 2, 1996, pp. 474–478.

7. For these statistics, see "Bu$ine$$ a$ U$ual: 1995 Campaign Contributions to House Members Continue to Grow," a research report by Citizen Action, Feb. 1996.

8. See Michael Weisskopf and David Maraniss, "Forging an Alliance for Deregulation," *The Washington Post*, March 12, 1995, p. A1.

9. For coverage of UPS safety problems, see Carey Gillam, "Did Ken Martin Have to Die?" *The Teamster*, Oct.–Nov. 1995, pp. 10–13.

10. For coverage of corporate contributions to Republican congressional campaigns, see John B. Judis, "The Contract with K Street," *The New Republic*, Dec. 4, 1995, pp. 18–25.

11. See "The Death of Machine Age Politics," editorial in *The New Democrat*, magazine of the Democratic Leadership Council, July–August 1995, p. 6.

12. See Michael Rothschild, "Beyond Repair: The Politics of the Machine Age Are Hopelessly Obsolete," *The New Democrat*, magazine of the Democratic Leadership Council, July–August 1995, p. 8.

5. *Changing Lives, Changing America*

1. For an account of the Feb. 1996 AFL-CIO Executive Council meeting, see David Moberg, "The New Union Label," *The Nation*, pp. 11–15.

2. For coverage of Justice for Janitors, see Michael J. Ybarra, "Jani-

tors' Union Uses Pressure and Theatrics to Expand Its Ranks," *The Wall Street Journal*, March 21, 1994, p. A1; "In Your Face!" *Union*, Service Employees International Union, fall 1994, pp. 7–9.

3. For coverage of organizing among poultry workers, see G. Paschal Zachary, "Signs of Revival: Some Unions Step Up Organizing Campaigns and Get New Members," *The Wall Street Journal*, Sept. 1, 1995, p. A1; Ronald Smothers, "Unions Try to Push Past Workers' Fears to Sign Up Poultry Plants in the South," *The New York Times*, Jan. 30, 1996, p. A10.

4. For coverage of the efforts by AFSCME and BUILD, see William Greider, "The Temporary Miracle: How One Good Job Becomes Three Lousy Ones," *Rolling Stone*, Aug. 19, 1993, pp. 32–33, 87; James Bock, "Alliance for a New Work Force," *The Baltimore Sun*, May 22, 1994, p. 18, and "Labor Leaders Preach and Preachers Urge Union Solidarity," *The Baltimore Sun*, May 23, 1994, p. 18; Marc V. Levine, "A Nation of Hamburger Flippers," *The Baltimore Sun*, July 31, 1994, p. 1E.

5. For an account of the Charlotte, N.C., discussion group, see Susan Dentzer, "Anti-Union, but Not Anti-Unity," *U.S. News & World Report*, July 17, 1995, p. 47.

6. See Lisa Oppenheim, "Women's Ways of Organizing: A Conversation with AFSCME Organizers Kris Rondeau and Gladys McKenzie," *Labor Research Review 18*, 1991, pp. 45–61.

7. For an account of the organizing drive at Harvard, see John Hoerr, "Solidaritas at Harvard," *The American Prospect*, summer 1993, pp. 67–83.

8. For a survey of union efforts on training, see "Labor's Key Role in Workplace Training," Markley Roberts and Robert Wozniak, AFL-CIO Economic Research Department, Sept. 1994.

9. For coverage of the Boeing strike and settlement, see Lawrence M. Fisher, "Union Rejects Boeing Offer," *The New York Times*, Oct. 7, 1995, sect. 1, p. 8; Peter T. Kilborn, "Labor's New Leaders Visit Boeing Strike," *The New York Times*, Nov. 13, 1995, p. A12; Timothy Egan, "Machinists End Boeing Strike, Declaring a Victory for Labor," *The New York Times*, Dec. 15, 1995, p. A41.

10. For gain-sharing in the steel industry, see Robert Kuttner,

"America Deserves a Raise," *The Washington Post,* Oct. 29, 1995, pp. C1, C6.

11. For coverage of labor-management cooperation at Levi Strauss, see Louis Uchitelle, "A New Labor Design at Levi Strauss," *The New York Times,* Oct. 13, 1994, p. D1, and Cara Metz, "Now We Can Speak Up," *UNITE!,* Jan.–Feb. 1996, pp. 16–18.

12. For the events in Billings, Montana, see Richard Cordtz, "Bigotry Busters," *Union,* Service Employees International Union, May–June 1995, p. 19.